Selected Poems

NATALYA GORBANEVSKAYA was born in Moscow in 1936. Expelled from Moscow University, she graduated from the Philology Department of Leningrad University. She was arrrested in 1968 for protesting against the Soviet-led invasion of Czechoslovakia. Gorbanevskaya now lives in Paris, where until 2001 she worked for the Russian émigré newspaper *Russkaya mysl*. She has published a number of poetry collections in Europe and the USA since leaving Russia.

DANIEL WEISSBORT co-founded the magazine *Modern Poetry in Translation* with Ted Hughes and edited it from 1965 to 2003. He is Emeritus Professor, University of Iowa, where he directed the MFA Program in Translation, and Honorary Professor in the Centre for Translation and Comparative Cultural Studies at the University of Warwick. He has published collections of poems and translations and edited several anthologies, most recently, with Valentina Polukhina, *An Anthology of Contemporary Russian Women Poets* (Carcanet, 2005).

VALENTINA POLUKHINA was born in Siberia and educated at Kemerovo, Tula and Moscow universities. Between 1962 and 1973 she taught at Moscow Lumumba University and from 1973 to 2001 she was Professor of Russian at Keele University. She has published on poets such as Akhmatova, Pasternak, Tsvetaeva, Khlebnikov and Mandelshtam, and is the author and editor of major studies of Joseph Brodsky. She has a particular interest in introducing Russian literature to English readers.

Also available from Carcanet Press

An Anthology of Contemporary Russian Women Poets,
edited by Valentina Polukhina and Daniel Weissbort

Alexander Blok, *Selected Poems*,
translated by Jon Stallworthy and Peter France

Joseph Brodsky, *Collected Poems in English*,
translated by Anthony Hecht, Howard Moss, Derek Walcott,
Richard Wilbur et al.

After Pushkin, edited by Elaine Feinstein

Marina Tsvetaeva, Bride of Ice: New Selected Poems, translated by
Elaine Feinstein

NATALYA GORBANEVSKAYA

Selected Poems

Translated with an introduction by
DANIEL WEISSBORT

With an interview by
VALENTINA POLUKHINA

CARCANET

First published in Great Britain in 2011 by
Carcanet Press Limited
Alliance House
Cross Street
Manchester M2 7AQ

Versions of 'Curses! Joy! They write themselves!', 'The savage cold of a Russian winter', 'Hold out a handful of snow', 'Make haste, enjoy the oblique caress of the rain, the sunlight', 'Drought, malevolent stepmother', 'It was not I saved Warsaw then, or Prague after' and 'Time to think' were first published in *Russian Poetry: The Modern Period*, edited by John Glad and Daniel Weissbort (Iowa University Press, 1978) and are included by kind permission of the publisher.

ISBN 978 1 84777 085 1

The publisher acknowledges financial assistance from Arts Council England

Supported by
**ARTS COUNCIL
ENGLAND**

Typeset by XL Publishing Services, Tiverton
Printed and bound in England by SRP Ltd, Exeter

Contents

SELECTED POEMS

From *Poberezhye* [Seaboard] (1956–66)

From *Angel derevianny* [Wooden Angel] (1967–71)

From *Tri tetradi stikhotvorenii* [Three Notebooks of Poems] (1972–4)

From *Pereletaya snezhnuyu granitsu* [Flying Over the Snowy Frontier] (1974–8)

From *Chuzhie kamni* [Alien Stones] (1979–82)

SELECTED POEMS

From *Poslednie stikhi togo veka* [Last Poems of the Last Century]
(1999–2000)

From *Krugi po vode* [Circles in the Water] (January 2006–August 2008)

Introduction

I wrote an introduction to an earlier selection of Natalya Gorbanevskaya's poetry published by Carcanet in 1972, with some additional materials, since the transcript of her trial and documents relating to her detention and obligatory 'treatment' in a prison psychiatric hospital had become available to me. I drew attention to the standard Soviet abuse of psychiatry, but also pointed out that this was not unprecedented in Russian history, as earlier regimes had used the threat of a diagnosis of insanity as a way of controlling rebelliousness; thus, under Catherine the Great, the aristocratic author and social critic Alexander Radishchev was arrested for his accurate depiction of socio-economic conditions in Russia, this earning him exile to Siberia. Radishchev was defined as insane and may well appear to have been so, to be challenging the overwhelming power of an autocratic state. The courageous demonstration in Red Square organised by Gorbanevskaya on 25 August 1968 revealed the abuse of power routinely practised by the Party-dominated Soviet state, including the use of psychiatric clinics as prisons where forced treatment was administered by personnel attached to and answerable to the KGB (political police). Gobanevskaya was eventually released and, like Joseph Brodsky, was expelled from the Soviet Union, taking up residence in Paris where she still lives and writes. For many years she was a contributing editor of the émigré newspaper *Russkaya mysl'* (Russian Thought). She did not cease to write poetry and has published many poetry collections.

While it was her activity as a dissident and civil rights activist that first brought her to my attention, I also believe that she is one of the most interesting contemporary poets writing in Russian. It seems to me that her approach to poetry is rather more traditional, perhaps, than that of poets remaining in Russia. But this may be partly due to the fact that the inflected Russian language lends itself to traditional techniques, especially with regard to rhyme, while the strong accent encourages the use of regular metre. Unlike Brodsky, whom she greatly admired and with whom she was associated,

Gorbanevskaya does however make use of *vers libre*; like Brodsky, she also expands the rhyming possibilities of Russian. When I met Brodsky in London, immediately after his expulsion from the Soviet Union in 1972, he asked me whether I would want my versions of Gorbanevskaya's poems to stand as a memorial to myself as a translator. I was not accustomed to thinking of translation in such exalted terms, but it transpired that what he had in mind was that I might have tried harder to imitate Gorbanevskaya's formal virtuosity, especially her use of rhyme. However, I was not and am not convinced, it still seeming to me that meaning is as important as the sometimes quite routine prosodic means employed to convey it, to preserve which faithfully, however, would necessitate radical semantic adjustments. I have generally resisted the contention that translation is a form of 're-writing', necessitating semantic as well as other adjustments. My choice of poems to translate has, accordingly, been restricted, in that poems which depend largely on sound tend to be excluded. Gorbanevskaya's work seems to me, on the whole, to be situated somewhere between the extremes. Certain of her poems I would regard as untranslatable (that is, untranslatable by myself), but so insistent are the pressures on her that an equivalent can often be found in English, even if Anglo-American historical experience, in our century, has been very different from the Russian.

I am grateful to Carcanet Press for being willing to revisit a poet who has continued to write poetry in her native language, despite having made her home in Paris, and to keep an eye on social and political developments in Russia, commenting acidly on them in her journalism and essays. It is probably true to say that political changes in the post-USSR world have again, ironically, rendered her work and that of other émigré poets almost invisible, since the literary world adheres to socio-economic realities.

The threat of official sanction may no longer exist, but Gorbanevskaya's recent poetry seems as clearly focused and as dedicated to human freedom – in the sense of freedom from political oppression – as it ever was. Her experiences of Soviet oppression have left a mark and she quite frequently evokes that earlier period, but, in general, her work has become more personal. It is, therefore, perhaps somewhat easier to come to terms with, though not necessarily to translate. What is evident is that her poetry is not just a political phenomenon; in this sense, her later work throws new light on her earlier work. Every poet has far more poems than see the light of day and Gorbanevskaya is quite prolific; although she also writes journalism, it does seem that for her the natural language of expression is verse. This will perhaps strike us as odd, since poetry is now usually seen as a marginal activity, poems being rare birds.

Gorbanevskaya's work is also imbued with a strong religious sensibility. She writes as a believer in divine revelation and the efficacy of religious observance, so that some of her poems read almost like prayers. This has, of course, to be contrasted with the Soviet context of official atheism, but there is more to it than political non-conformism or contrariness. It seems likely that it is religion that has sustained her in a difficult life. Dylan Thomas says somewhere that poetry is also a prayer. There is something remorselessly literal about Gorbanevskaya's writing, in its utter directness, whether about the oppressive state or her personal relations. She brings to ordinary human relations what has been learnt in an ultra-hard school.

How relevant, one is tempted to ask, in view of her commitments, is her recent work to current political realities? I believe that the tradition of Russian poetry has been preserved precisely by poets such as Gorbanevskaya and Brodsky, continuing stubbornly to write in their native language, the only language of poetry for them, while living in an alien linguistic and cultural environment. The exposure to another linguistic culture has given their work a strange depth or multi-dimensionality, relevant in a mixed society in which movement between linguistic universes is almost routine. I am not qualified or able to comment on the extent to which exposure to French literature and language has affected Gobanevskaya's perspective. It is true, in any case, that French and Russian cultures have, for two centuries, had much to do with one another, and there is a sophisticated Russian émigré culture in France, especially in Paris. For Gorbanevskaya, this émigré world is thus not a completely alien world. The habits of youth have remained with her, and her work is politically engaged and contemporary.

The profession of poet, in the West, is financially insecure, and Gorbanevskaya supplements it with political commentary. My meetings with her suggest that she is as feisty now as when she first appeared on the scene, reading at a poetry festival in London alongside the likes of W.H. Auden and Robert Graves, where, to her evident embarrassment, her heroic life was celebrated in song by the folk-singer Shusha.

In this second collection, I have focused more than before on Gorbanevskaya's poetry rather than on her predicament and the ordeal she suffered, writing poetry in a world that does not value the art highly. She has continued to write poetry, thus validating, as it seems to me, my earlier perception. She evidently feels impelled also to participate in the continuing civil rights movement in Russia, insofar as it is possible to do so from a distance. The fact is that she has not been forgotten, so significant was her example. Her poetry, not surprisingly, still recalls those moments when her personal history and that of her country intersected, but Gorbanevskaya remains as concerned as ever about the fate of Russia. I have included in this book a prose piece and an interview, conducted by Valentina Polukhina, in which the poet discusses her life and commitment. This makes it inappropriate to add anything more here.

As regards the poetry, it is hardly necessary to point out yet again that translation is usually no better than an approximation. I have taken a few liberties but, on the whole, have tried to remain close to the literal rendering. Valentina Polukhina's collaboration has made this project possible and she has pointed out the extent to which Gorbanevskaya has been influenced by the inimitable Khlebnikov, as also by the equally inimitable Joseph Brodsky. In my renderings, Gorbanevskaya appears more of a free-verse poet than she is, virtually all her poems being rigorously rhymed and metrically regular. I have attempted to give some sense of this, but it is hard to do so without gross distortion of normal English usages. Much more could be said, but I do not wish to interpose between the reader and the material my own reflections and doubts.

Daniel Weissbort
London, 2010

Note on the Text

The poems have been selected and arranged chronologically. They have been taken from several collections; the date ranges given after the book titles indicate the dates between which the poems in that book were composed. Some of the poems were published in earlier versions in *Selected Poems* by Natalya Gorbanevskaya with a transcript of her trial and papers relating to her detention in a prison psychiatric hospital, edited and introduced by Daniel Weissbort (Oxford: Carcanet Press, 1972); *Post-war Russian Poetry*, edited by Daniel Weissbort (Harmondsworth: Penguin, 1974); and *Russian Poetry: The Modern Period*, edited by John Glad and Daniel Weissbort (Iowa City: University of Iowa Press, 1978). There is a small selection of Gorbanevskaya's poetry in *An Anthology of Russian Women Poets*, edited by Valentina Polukhina (Manchester: Carcanet Press, 2005).

For an account of Natalya Gorbanevskaya's literary beginnings, readers are advised to consult the 1972 Carcanet volume.

From *Poberezhye* [Seaboard]
(1956–66)

On reading Ray Bradbury's *Fahrenheit 451*

Clever, so clever,
such clever people,
not to be blamed.
Such clever people,
almost wise.

Carbonised dust-jackets
of books unread by me.
Carbonised dust-jackets.
And an illiterate stoker.

Such clever people:
– Burn! Burn!
They claimed these books
were his enemy.

People access the ash:
– So, rummage in good and evil.
People have access to ash:
– Look for happiness there.

I sift through the ash,
soot-covered to the elbow,
sift through ash.
Not one letter left.

Such clever people,
They've thought of everything,
so others need
think of nothing.

1956

★

The fire in the oven's barely out,
logs ticking over.
The hour of truth has not yet struck,
the crime's not been expunged.

The day of judgement has not arrived,
trumpeted over the sleeping hills
to the cities, gifts still being brought
from the impoverished villages.

Chill blue smoke, over the house,
suspended in the limpid air,
and to those he doesn't know, through those he does
the Lordly angel makes known his word:

The crime has not yet been expunged,
the hour of truth has not yet struck.
logs in the stove still ticking over,
although the fire's already out.

1956

Note
The date indicates that this was written at the time of the Soviet invasion
of Hungary, a moment of great disillusionment, especially for young people
in the USSR.

Morning. A lively wind. The woods
agitated, each tree a spindle.
From the hair, tangled webs.
Each tree, an entire forest.
Each tree, a home.
Under each tree, our home,
with table and couch:
pale webs,
tangled in the hair,
clinging, clutching,
fragile twigs,
enmeshing the cones.

Good morning.
Let's with a sleepy hand
disengage the webs,
brush off grass wisps,
dry the tears on your cheeks.
No need to hurry,
not the last time.
In the wind-tossed forest
a tearless eye.

1960

★

Concerto for orchestra

Bartók, listen to what you've written!
Like beating a rusty frying-pan: rat-tat-tat,
like mountains mounting mountains,
rivers circling themselves,
hands lengthening into tinkling reeds,
long-muzzled boats,
nudging white landing-stages.
And the musician of the year before last,
much admired, to judge from the price of tickets,
sitting and frowning;
    but however many pans you scrape this rust off,
    it's always the same: noise,
    racket, not the real thing.
Bartók, just listen to what you've written!
Like ink spilt on a collar,
knocking teeth out with a rusty pan.
Again, the orchestra plays, under direction,
and the public leaps up, and makes for the cloakroom.
What a cheek! And, after, 'tee-tum' you intone,
thank You, Lord, for sending them a lucid interval.

1962

★

My Fortinbras, poor brother,
behold this, my Denmark,
sprung from my side,
in my very image.

And this, my game, behold,
yours now,
the path of virtue, with endless obstacles,
mystery of being.

Take all that was mine,
or stop, wait,
change your mind,
Not yet king,
depart, silence the drums,
decline this role.

                                                    1962

                        ★

I'll fill the oil lamp.
How lovely you are, my land,
suspended in the gleaming heights,
a basket woven by me,
with the whole universe in it.

How lovely, my land,
like that other, by the bay,
that half-mad willow,
offering its branches freely,
out of millennial love.

My land, my light and strength,
my destiny, how fine,
how dark, my star,
and Russia's misty name
I was born to bear, from birth.

                                                    1963

                        ★

Why speak of disaster or beauty,
when, naked as the thief upon the cross,
the body, oblivious yet joyful,
wishes to be deceived.

Who laments and weeps,
crossing the snowy frontier,
where an icy wind
chills the bright surface of a well.

And this unearthly merging of passions,
this breathless parting of hands,
as on the cross, the snap of bones,
as at the stake, the crackle and the blaze.

1964

★

I do not chase rhymes, seeking glory,
nor you, everything up for sale!
Search as you might, hop, don't look round,
like a sparrow on the Hermitage roof.

A battle-tested sparrow,
into the indomitable wind,
over this absurd, wide world,
like a boat among mountainous waves.

1964

★

Don't touch me! I scream at passers-by
who scarcely notice me.
Cursing other people's rooms,
I linger in anterooms.

But who'll knock a window through?
or hold out his hand?
I am roasting over a slow fire.

                                        1964

                    ★

Nothing – neither fear
nor stiffening before the execution,
I lay my head on the scrubbed block,
as on a lover's shoulder.

Roll, curly one, over the scrubbed boards,
don't splinter those parted lips,
the boards bruise your temples,
the trumpet still sounds in your ear,

polished copper dazzles,
horses' manes toss –
what bliss to die on such a day!
.   .   .   .
Another morning and scarce a glimmer.

And in the dimness, half awake –
either some old fever or some new apocrypha –
my lover's shoulder
still has the tang of pine.

                                        1965

                    ★

Unfinished poem

To A. Roginsky

Already past midnight, and
every other street-lamp lit;
wander about the town until
dawn lights the sky.

Night has erased the year,
the age from the buildings' facades,
the town, bleak as an allotment,
but also like the Ark,

floating and now entering
the chill of dawn,
and between the windows, near the gate,
the age and time appear,

and you come to yourself, weeping,
on the bridge, over the Yauza river.

1965

★

And mingling tears with the rain's sweetness,
tasting the salt of eyelashes,
I am happy. Really? Rouse yourself,
the stars still wrapped in damp clouds,

and in the dark heaven, only zones of moisture
leave visible traces,
iniquitous courts having banished
the moonlight into distant exile.

1965

On Twelfth Night, sings the cricket,
a January Monday,
and the pealing of the bells,
floating among the snow-hills,
barely, barely touches them
with its wing.

On Twelfth Night, the cricket sings;
my visitor is silent,
and the pealing of the bells
drowns in the snow,
melts in the sky,
in cornerless space.

But by the stove in a corner,
the crickets chirp, like homunculi,
while the bells peal, melt and drown,
but touch us, brush us,
with their wings.

1965

★

Don't destroy me, Lord,
losing me in a game of chance,
sending me out to roam the world,
believing in nothing.

You who bestrode the waves,
as if it were dry land,
don't dispatch me, staffless,
through the sift of earthly sufferings.

from POBEREZHYE

Son of Man, who burdened me
with a yoke and bell, free me not
to wander the icy night,
where my soul must freeze.

1965

★

Love, what nonsense,
what bird-brained foolishness,
when it's already too late
to spare or pity me,
keep silent, silent,
not inflating red cheeks
in the familiar song of finches,

where the poet,
randomly traducing themes,
imitates bird-cries,
sighs and whispers,
lips astir, infiltrating
the dark communion of fish,
and finally, a subterranean hum.

Love from every part,
food for verse,
or the foolish song of mindless goldfinches,
the crowing of roosters,
keep silent, cease your babble.
Let your hand stroke my cheek.
How hot the fingers,
and low the ceilings!

1965

★

Denying love,
to fall a victim to it,
lifting the dark from words,
like hands from a face.

and to see the burst of light
over town and woods
like a *Kyrie Eleison*,
or a March-Day slogan,

a Mozart chorus
over the ice rumble,
like blissful cold flowing
from the white hills.

1966

★

Joyous Mozart with an oar,
grieving Mozart with a sail.
My tear-free cheekbones grieve,
the ocular music dulls.

Bitter, the mid-winter warmth,
immersing me in a snowdrift.
Joyous Mozart with a sail,
grieving Mozart with a wing.

Yet neither any headway makes –
Splash oar, crack sail!

1966

★

To Yu. Galanskov

In the madhouse,
wring your palms,
beat your brow against the wall,
as if face-down into a snow-drift.

There, in the murky turbulence,
smiling broadly,
Russia stumbles,
as into a mirror.

For her son,
a dose of stelazin;
for herself –
a Potyomsky escort.

1966

Notes
Stelazin: a powerful tranquilliser. Potyomsky: from Pot'ma, a place in
Mordova which was the site of Soviet concentration camps.

★

You are my grief. Laugh then!
A liquid moon twists me around.

But that's not why I gulp back tears,
like a mouthing fish, swallowing the chill air.

Smile, my grief, pass me on the path
where the frenzied woodpecker taps,
and the mossy tower totters
on its hen's leg.

1966

★

In my own twentieth century,
where are more dead than coffins for them,
my miserable, forever
unshared love,

among these Goya images,
is anxious, faint, absurd,
as after the howl of jets,
the trump of Jericho.

1966

★

You howl, you weep *ad lib*
on the green grass,
and return to your slavery,
mind numbed.

You howl, weep, gulp back
bitter tears,
roll down steep slope
into the nettles.

And again return. How long
to continue?
Your palms tingling with burrs,
sharpen your pencil,

scribble a line,
on your wrist, scribble,
spot a blade of grass
with a drop of blood.

1966

Feverish and sweating,
I am rambling about you,
long desired and un-loved
who's dear, who's not.
I drop into an oblivious, nether world,
where only the body speaks,
while the wretched soul stays under lock and key.

And in those depths, that darkness,
you're like a mirage,
and my voice calls softly.
The hot pillow against my cheek,
the cannon booming at noon,
a deafness gripping my throat,
a bitterness inundating my eyes.

1966

From *Angel derevianny* [Wooden Angel]
(1967–71)

Just music, nothing else –
neither joy, nor peace,
in suffering's glassy sea,
music – the one saving grace,

for an hour or so,
with neither yesterday, nor tomorrow;
in the midst of winter, a flute sings,
like the oriole, of summer.

But this momentary oblivion ends;
the human bird falls silent,
and barefoot over shards,
I re-enter the blizzard's sombre space.

A star, an enchanting sonnet,
nothing to beguile you any more.
'Sleep peacefully!' but silently exclaim:
'No peace!'

1967

What is forever, what does 'forever' mean?
In an antique clock water drips,
in another, sand pours,
but my alarm clock aims at the temple

and wakes me – this time, forever –
from the brief, coloured dream
me, you, all of us, my friend,
for an eternity, for new eternal suffering.

1967

★

Preparing again to prolong his mortal span,
cut short by the soothsayer's word,
the prophet Oleg rejected the fatal horse.
Again, the prince shed tears over the skull,
from which the serpent, chortling,
had slithered.

Even with a hundred arms, mouths, faces,
meeting a mendacious madman,
no use putting questions.
All bones rest in the Lord's hands.
The scoop brims and foams,
echoing the hissing snake.

1967

As brought to bay, the deer falls,
crushing the blood-stained grass,
the exhausted day hurries towards night,
a blind fugitive into reprisal's arms.

O times, customs! Amid
the deaths, the empty immortalities,
forgetting, in her madness, names,
she rants of Hamlet or Laertes…

1967

★

Curses! Joy! They write themselves!
Words shift, like mountains,
and, like a moth, I flutter
between the lines.

Only yesterday, at the approach
of unbelief and sadness,
as desperate as a stranded fish,
I gasped.

And now, each little stream
burbles, like a goldfinch.
The river flowing, its speech
strumming against my cheek.

Goldfinch! Cuckoo! Starling!
In this female throat
a vernal breeze floats
between the lines.

1967

from ANGEL DEREVIANNY

*

Darling, darling, astonished,
I see, above you,
a wooden angel,
with a wooden trumpet,

silently sounding,
a voice of desiccated wood,
and I do not hear the word
uttered by your desiccated lips.

The other side of the thin partition,
a trumpet voice moans;
the angel flares, subsides,
a coal dropped in the corner.

The trumpet dies,
tears dry in the eye.
Rain streams down every twig,
the astonished angel is silent.

1967

*

Hold out a handful of snow,
I kiss your hand,
tell no one of these days,
I neither weep nor grieve.

Bullfinches in snowdrifts.
How warm your eyelashes!
A handful of snow,
tomtits along the aspens.

And the light, autumnal snow,
pricked by grass blades.
I scald myself with
a handful of snow.

                                            1967

                    ★

Forgive, forgive,
always forgive me,
that I cannot say good-bye,

stammering as I run,
moaning, sighing,
waving a handkerchief.

I do not speak, recalling
what the tall grass felt like,
and how it tasted.

                                            1968

                    ★

My love, in what region
– already I do not know you –
what herbs are you gathering?
and over a stream, by means of a log,
folding the wings, on which
you hurry to answer a call?

Your forgotten sister,
brought neither by wind or fire –
sings in a dark prison-cell,
she, too, folding her wings,
falling silent only when
the transport leaves for Presnya.

January 1970, Butyrskaya Prison

Note
Presnya: Moscow's transit prison.

★

The train's French horn sweeps on,
an unattainable myth.
A flame trickles through the bars,
worlds eclipsed.

The horn sweeps into the night,
playing the tracks.
How am I ever to reach
that rainy platform!

Sleepless, deserted,
empty without me
tattered clouds settling, like letters,
onto your concrete,

puddles with full-stops:
hooks and tails;
voices ringing out
after the departed train.

July–September 1970, Butyrskaya Prison

The savage cold of a Russian winter,
my devastated pedestal!
The agonising pain of this pose,
myself seeking warmth, a piece of southern stone.

Pygmalion has no love for Galatea,
someone's easy laughter holding him in sway.
In impotent silence, I rage,
bleeding from the nose, gulping the frozen snow.

February 1971, Kazan

From *Tri tetradi stikhotvorenii*
[Three Notebooks of Poems]
(1972–4)

My Moscow, a waxen board,
poems walk on the first snow,
my *ennui*, which I cannot hide,
but do not press to my pale brow.

And watermarks showing through,
the page dries the tears shed by me.
And each night prison-trains leave
the Kazan Station for the East.

★

Make haste, enjoy the oblique caress of the rain, the sunlight,
while the earth's still moist, the sky un-parched,
while the Neva and Onega run deep between their banks
and damp powder hasn't yet fallen from the gun.

Drought, malevolent stepmother
of the fading petal,
scent of the East in dandelion seeds,
even waves of sand.

Before nightfall, read what's written
on the tablet suspended from above…
Virtuous mother, three-handed defender,
brush off the dried blood, drying on your brow.

★

It was not I saved Warsaw then, or Prague after,
not I, my guilt's irredeemable,
my house hermetically sealed and cursed,
house of evil, sin, treachery and crime.

And chained by these everlasting invisible chains to it,
I'll find joy and venom in this dreadful house,
in a dark, smoky corner, inebriated, wretched,
where my people lives, guiltless and godless.

Investigating the herring head
the cubist surpassed the poor Dutchmen:
clouds of *makhorka*, starvation nightmares,
leaflets nutritionally smelling of paste,
with the pre-dawn lists of murders.

Feverish, you'd not dream up the like.
In a small stove burning senseless Brockhaus
issuing a warning; 'I'm not coming tomorrow'.
Reap your fate and your turn,
as in a line for fish-rations.

These years, hunger and years
(obsequious memory is like a mop),
mopped by snowstorm, and the dawn of freedom,
bared teeth, lifted by arches,
where the spirit is hard-pressed, and the flesh freezes.

Notes
Makhorka: an inferior brand of tobacco. Brockhaus: Brockhaus and Efron
is the main Russian-language encyclopaedic dictionary, 86 volumes,
published in Imperial Russia (1890–1906).

From *Pereletaya snezhnuyu granitsu*
[Flying Over the Snowy Frontier]
(1974–8)

Time to think
not of fleshly delights
and to scorn even spiritual pleasures.

Time, grain by grain, to count through
your hoard of bitterness
and make an amulet of it.

Time, my friend, time!

★

Decrepit Europe, your second childhood looming,
to whom will you leave your legacy
of a last tavern and bordello,
and a Charter of Freedom. It was not madness

impelled your earls and barons,
settling their nerves with wine,
tested in battle, not knowing
who was right, who had lost...

Poor Europe, my cemetery verses
are proof of a powerlessness,
irreparable love to the end,
a last grimace of the face,

yourself, marked with a network of slits
of trenches, when soldiers don't matter,
but there's freedom for the breeze,
for trucks and armoured cars.

★

Do not chase phantoms,
or snatch at emptiness,
in the cloud of deception,
you'll not catch a swallow in flight.

Or out-sing the nightingale,
or build an owl's nest
by daylight, or release
the language's hidden power.

Words will not become heavens,
as wood is not to be made of grass,
brought in by sleighs, as in the olden times
firewood to the yard.

Obviously from the forest. And you'll not utter
creation in the yard, in the grass
the creeping creature you'll wash only jam off
the cheek – as off the sleeve
you'll brush away a tear and smear
the second one, fulfilling the Commandment.

As in Moscow tears are not trusted, so here
('here' is not there, but an attempt is made to find words!).
Only the clock ticks on and on,
as though it wanted to be a word-hoard.

My dear, what's happening,
when the hour doesn't arrive,
when the hand sticks, unable to move,
and time twitching in the same place,
is unable to rise
one millimetre… Like a windless sail,
I faint in your palms,
invisible, undreamed, distant
in the complete revolution of a clock's hands
from me, as once upon a time, as *then*.

From *Chuzhie kamni* [Alien Stones]
(1979–82)

This truth is a lie,
this prose, written rhythmically,
this butter, accepting the knife
like the fulfilment of a prayer.

This heat turning chill,
but the death of the thermometer,
the best of coolness,
an icy draught in hell.

This truth, I insist on,
don't, don't believe it,
don't test it, with a knife pinning
the tender throat to the wall.

★

To Czesław Miłosz

At that time, I fell for foreign poems,
hissing so others scowl: 'Hissing…'
And thence, probably, much flowed
for me, some of it not good, some may be good.

Now I'm an inveterate translator, a professional,
endlessly rustling through Dahl's dictionary,
noting the chirp of Russian words
and muttering, as over a book of divination.

But thank me or God – I don't know whom,
not chance or error, whispering outside the Paris dark
I'm still uncertain before typing
the translation on my typewriter.

Not to myself, nor to God, not to chance, or the vocation –
to language itself, are due my love-declarations.

★

To A.D. Sakharov

He looked around, and his soul…
And the orchestra rumbles, stifling the wounded chest.
And a Lenin-like gesture, a projector, a fumble,
muffling, stifling, bending.

Through all of us passed a burst of fire
from Lenin's armoured car,
and if we were alive, it wasn't all that much,
continuing, all the same, for a while.

And until speech neither decaying nor petrifying,
distinguishing us from the beast,
through orchestral salvoes, a volley of marches,
no time to bother about vocal cords.

He looked about, and his soul…
And so did another, wounded,
a third making his way by touch,
making good the temporal links.

*

The untilled field is hemmed in the bonfires.
You run around, gesticulating,
as if a vein were constricted
by a tourniquet, face bloodless,
police-raids awaiting their turn,
a reflection playing on a rifleman's gun.
The playfulness ending, bonfires lit
licking rank, autumnal weeds,
and corroding the surface of wounds,
indentations, scarred the bare,
virgin soil of burrow and gully.
Nowhere to hide, neither in sleep
nor insanity, nor within the forest's wall,
beyond the fires, and a wad of thorns
ready. And back-sights sweeping.
You're an object, a target, safe for now.
Darkness already turning to a shadow,
night making itself visible.
The heart hammers at the ribs like a flail.
Wonders visible neither in front
nor in the rear, nor anywhere;
from above, only crows call.
Morning rain beating upon the cinders,
the sky suspended over empty fields,
like a filthy strip of gauze, a cry of pain
dropping like mist over the distant woods.

*

A year of dire predictions.
Fortune-tellers, fearing recriminations,
go underground. Near Kazan,
calves are born, soldered together.
Beyond the Urals, the marsh swallowing an oil-rig;

with an unprecedentedly fiery burst,
all Kamchatka's volcanoes erupting simultaneously;
on Presnya, plum-sized cockroaches.
News of these monstrous happenings multiplied,
hardly concealed by the press.
Horror intensified, pity became pointless,
almost a formality. In Okhta,
a mother abandoned her child on a tram;
claws ripped wordlessly through nothing;
in a hut a nine-year-old suicide was discovered.
No one able to figure out why.
Appeals for order were constantly issued,
printed, broadcast over the radio,
but all the people heard were
rumours, rumours, nothing but...

★

It got warmer and warmer
and then got cold, again.
In the stove, a flame flickered;
in the throat, hunger.

Ashes, dust, specks,
merging like microbes.
In our ice-age, grass blades –
how goes it?

Hard to forget what happened,
what got burnt, or poured out,
incinerated, or obliterated,
destroying those fragile beams?

Does it hurt to harden,
like a handful of melted wax,
so only slaked lime might settle
in heart, in throat...

from CHUZHIE KAMNI

From *Peremennaya oblachnost'*
[Alternating Clouds]
(1982–3)

This little clay bird –
is myself.
Angels are used to
singing a ditty,

to the rhythm of rain and snow,
to a song singing,
then flinging me
against a wall.

But these colourful fragments
– rubbish, trash, and fumes –
not falling, nor shall they fall
silently.

Angels are used to
singing and stopping.
But unstable as hoar-frost,
the spirit inhales cold clay,
wheezing, not wearying.

From *Gde i kogda* [Where and When]
(1983–5)

A poor fly in amber
didn't mean to wing it.
The Orwellian calendar
has ended.

The poor fly in amber
can neither breathe nor move.
And on the plank-bed in January
it's so tight, one can hardly move.

Flames quietly lick the Orwellian
cover in the stove.
The poor fly sings,
but no one hears.

★

Epitaph

(On the death of Vadim Delaunay)

Closer than a brother, the first and youngest
of us seven, whence no return.
Sweeter than sweet life, whereas there were seven,
hacking, digging the frozen earth?

To fall asleep that way, and to wake, detached from the earth,
beyond exile, KPP, barbed-wire...
beyond the thorny stars. Pray for us,
offer your fraternal help.

Notes
Vadim Nikolaevich Delaunay (1947–83) was a Russian poet and dissident,
participant in the 1968 Red Square demonstration against the military
suppression of the 'Prague Spring'. The seven dissidents organised the
demonstration; Delaunay and Pavel Litvinov were actually holding the
banner with the words 'For Your Freedom and Ours'. The seven
demonstrators were arrested and tried. Delaunay defiantly stated that the
five minutes of freedom were worth the years in prison awaiting him. KPP:
Frontier Control Point (*Kontrol'no-propusknoi punkt*).

From *Sed'maya kniga* [Seventh Book]
(1985–90)

Notes for a discussion on statistics

Not to dispute it; a superfluous million
of honoured, tormented, forgotten individuals –
just a number. A million tears
haven't merged to cause a flood,
or melted the permafrost.
Let's suppose, history foresees
this million names and disinters them,
but in the world's four capitals,
who'll read so weighty a book,
heavy as a telephone directory.
Who'll buy it? You may entertain yourself
with abacus beads, but a million tears
won't thaw the permafrost.

★

Where the pollen crowds
and midges rise
to the level of the face,
holding their masked ball,

to rip off a mask
is like smashing a doll,
where you cannot visit
or love me,

where the silvery dark
is like a fir-tree
on Christmas eve,
sinking into a quagmire,

where singing's like lying,
crying out, like betraying,
where the brushwood road trembles,
like a string of beads,

making one lose one's footing,
hand trembling –
that's about all there is to
a moth-clustered ceiling.

From *I ya zhila-byla* [Once Upon a Time]
(1992–4)

'The fate of her children doesn't concern her.'

This phrase from the experts' diagnosis
resounds, like a silvery clarinet,
losing its menace,
but not fading.

It's good when my sons are breathing in the next room
and it's not cell-mates;
good to wake up, without groaning,
gazing into a non-venomous future;

good not to feed the brain's convolution:
whether something is amiss: you're you or not,
breathing from under the ruins
the ashes of those who – O, God! – will not be back.

★

Waiting for the end,
don't crowd over the threshold.
All may inherit a space
in Our Father's house.

Don't imbibe someone else's head,
fresh shavings, tar;
beyond the stifling dark,
there's room and time.

A six-digit tag takes flight,
with moist agitation,
on someone's
lilac-smeared palm.

Don't stuff words in,
languishing mutely;
in Our Father's house,
the song is endless.

From *Nabor* [Type-setting]
(1994–6)

And my friend was sold for a bushel of wheat,
our God was betrayed for thirty kopeks,
and Christ's shroud was pierced, and sweaty,
and the thief, as well, the river-pirate, the pedlar,

and all situations and circumstances,
and all personages from the One Above to the smallest one,
fragments and reflections of The Effulgence,
on grey clouds, dove-grey rocks.

★

My head's badly arranged,
birthing not thoughts, just words,
not self-generated –
that's about it!

The seed, dropped into flesh,
to ripen in its own good time,
bursts from the temporal,
generating bones.

Unmilled flour
coagulating into a martyr,
mouthing, with a butted tongue,
extracted, as by an empty ladle.

The doctor peers at the x-ray
of the inside of my head:
for my sins,
trash mostly.

★

This groan of ours, this wail,
this sob of a dactylic clause,
or howl of the begging crowds,
hungering for Lazarus,

is called song,
i.e., a poem,
fed by mould
and crushed glass.

From *Novye vos'mistishiya* [New Eight-line] (1996)

7.
The Russian language
has lost its instrument.
Hands wipe themselves
on overalls,
the language, moving its lips,
cannot get used to the fact
that Joseph has died,
failing to brush away its tears.

Note
'…has lost its instrument': a reference to Joseph Brodsky's statement that
a poet is the instrument of language, not the other way around.

From *Kto o chyom poyot* [Who Sings What]
(April 1996–September 1997)

Exegi monumentum

1.
A crude tuft
of what's left of the wick,
I raised to myself
a monument of wax.
Soot drifts off,
and the pedestal cools,
but, before melting,
it lit someone's path.

From *13 vos'mistishii i eshche 67 stikhotvorenii*
[13 Eight-liners and Sixty-seven More Poems]
(1997–9)

The Russian 'no'
in a foreign land;
I do not call, or yearn, or weep.
A rehash-negative,
resounding my swallowing
failure and my ill luck.

Don't, please, don't, don't, I beg you,
write or call.
No calls, e-mails, or letters.
Don't call or feel sorry.
The sky gets numb
when split by a wedge of cranes.

From *Poslednie stikhi togo veka*
[Last Poems of the Last Century]
(1999–2000)

My drink's neither hot, nor weak,
my fate settling into the sediment,
my hands not holding the pen,
my evenings not well-illuminated,
my midnights neither bright nor warm.
Nobody needs what I've got,
fingers descend onto
the keyboard.

*

He Who let us sin and badmouth Him
will not desert us, whatever the weather.
Don't dice to see how things may turn out,
but refrain from evil, even if unable to praise.

*

Time to stop
hovering, turning
around whatever-may-be,

time to bid the hand farewell,
like a mitten
dropped in the snow.

Time to re-forge experience
into a whisper,
to the rustle of dry, fallen leaves,
final truths, prickly as thorns.

★

Don't fear or grieve,
or let despair overwhelm you.
No one knows the day, the hour,
when, obedient to the Leadership's command
your guardian-angel will fold his wings.

No one knows the day, the hour,
when you'll emerge from the guard's hands
and like a white-winged magpie,
fall silent and sigh.
And the world will be more fearful, and older.

★

I don't see, hear, sensing
the brocade only by touch;
add to my funeral trappings
an already-yellowing
newspaper file,

did I dedicate myself,
under no illusion that body and mind
were ancestrally linked,
however frailly.

★

We live — at times,
and in between,
years pass
in awful or sweet

dreams.
Is someone counting
the pits and bumps
that wake us?

★

Telegraph Lane.
A black Volga,
in pursuit,
mounts the pavement:
a dream of '69.

Note
Telegraph Lane: a street in Moscow, which had a post-office in it.

*

Blessed is the epic poet,
with a sufficiency of breath
not to gulp
in mid-word…

*

On the long, long rue Vaugirard
nothing of interest,
aside from its length,
but the gracious city
tosses on either side,
in the heat-haze
of the brick-flow.

You gave up for lost
your long, long life,
but once in the long street,
outside your home,
you revive – not out of dogma,
but because you remember childhood places,
the short Neglinka,
the endless ring-road.

Note
Neglinka [Street]: a street in the centre of Moscow.

*

There she is, myself,
I go – we'll go – they went,
in the waterfall flocks of Naiads
echo.

Here is that, towards which,
crossing ditches, over pot-holes
came cloaks, loose
garments, flapping shirts.

And here we are, within Him,
clumsy, in the word of the proverb,
like a flame, in the waterfall,
the water staggering in mid-air.

★

But I was always
everyone's contemporary,
and, like water,
followed all the bends in the river.

And reached the sea,
deprived of rights, like everyone,
neither first nor ninth wave
passing me by.

One wave to another I say:
'What are we waiting for?
Time for the upper parts, too,
to be moistened by rain.'

Note
'Everyone's contemporary': in a well-known poem Osip Mandelstam
claimed to be nobody's contemporary.

★

SELECTED POEMS

Man, made in God's image,
you invented the bus for everyone
(not just me).
And I, also in his image, enter,
like and unlike the rest,
and present my pass,

a permit to mutter unintelligibly
incomprehensible to the French folk,
even to myself.
Leave your circuitous route
my six-wheeled *percheron*,
go as you will.

★

Hey, comrade lords,
on the ship!
The shore, floating away,
has moved towards the land.

We are possessionless,
naked among the waves,
just a pinch of salt
doled out in the sky,

a mere spoonful
in the ocean-cup,
a hundred grammes,
to be sipped by each,

under the sniffed-at
patched sleeve,
from the Holy Spirit,
a fireproof shirt.

★

Notes of a Cold War veteran

And bowler-hatted Churchill,
like some film comic,
with a waffle-like cigar,
looks around sharply.
We shivered, wept bitterly,
when the *Luftwaffe* deposited
its deadly cargo on his island.

Later, things turned around,
for better or worse.
Are we the allies of allies
or simply capitulationists?
At the memorable table,
they sit, as in stalls or puddles.
And prisoners sit in cells
from Yalta to Archangel.

From A to Z, relying on Fulton,
or the atomic bomb,
a Third World War, etc.
A ban on weeping
at least on noisy lamentations.
All that remains is to knock
our heads on the Wall.

★

And as children,
we're trapped in a net,
snares, nooses.
And to us, with a book, lamp-lit,
a thermometer in the armpit,
moths descended.

One day, we'll be asked,
where the wind carried us,
where we were rushing full-tilt,
into what kid's game,
what sorcerer, snare...
Where should we go?

★

And sacred inspiration,
commas, commas,
the spirit, dream-gripped,
another semi-colon,
and, passionate as Spain,
over obstacles, punctuation marks,
Pegasus galloping, in spite of all,
towards his peaceful stall.

★

10 = 9

(In memory of the Oberiuty)

...they should use iambs...

Where, in the aureole of black suns,
of a verb like things, over-filling themselves,
they joked like a Gascogne native,
galloping through the Russian snows,
there a gold coin waited for trochees,
a gold coin for free verse,
nine grammes, a bullet's weight.

Note
'The Oberiuty': poets belonging to OBERIU, the Society of Real Art
(1926–31), which included Daniil Kharms, Nikolai Zabolotsky and
Alexander Vvedensky among its core members.

Words float either here or there, scurrying,
like a flock of alarmed ducks,
the poem bristles, by a white flour mill,
swallows scatter, like leaflets.

★

A citizen?
So, live independently.
A poet?
So, travel the world,
embrace humanity,
with both arms,
bringing light and shade,
but making sure
it doesn't get blown out.

Note
This poem alludes to Pushkin's and Nekrasov's poems on the poet's role.

★

From Pindemonti

It has the feel and taste of a log,
right, left,
to be discussed.
The re-won right
to shake the poor air free,
to dance in the arena
of an open square,
where yesterday

people were burned
in the plague and at sea.

Note
This poem refers to Pushkin's poem of the same title.

★

You realise, don't you,
what I'm saying?
You'll not be telling us
this is just a product of the mind?
I listen, fear and see,

both the density and rarity of speech,
loaded onto these chance shoulders,
as a soldier, summoned to the *veche*,
quits the field of battle.

Note
Veche: a popular assembly in medieval Russian towns.

★

And at thirty-three
I encountered, not misfortune
but history. Strange
to be cutting, not a door or a window through,
but a skylight,
so closely barred, at that,
that the clouds, through it,
look like links in chains.

★

Words are out?
Well, what's the use?
Tuck them in a suitcase,
shove that under a couch.

No sighs, but deep breathing,
No 'ah's, or 'oh's,
no sighing, moaning
when offended, or insulted.

Don't cry,
don't fit yourself for a coffin,
but proceed like a shoe,
like a bean or straw.

★

I read the list of ships...

In Nakhodka, a crowded place,
where people barge one another,
did he remember, lying on a bunk,
the duration of vowels,

orioles in the forest
the supreme ordeal,
the dying, in Homer,
those archaic sails...

Notes
The poem's title refers to Osip Mandelstam's well known poem 'I read the
list of ships...'. Nakhodka: a port-city in the far east of Russia, to which
Mandelstam was exiled.

★

On the snow-frontier, eyelashes freeze to a column,
to the stalks of last year's veronica and dodder,
tearfully, I watch the migrating birds
and, like Petka to Chapayev, pose idiotic questions.

Not incorporated into Mendeleyev's table of elements,
not listening to gesticulating magi, cops, maestros.
I'll jump higher than my own petty height,
and bash my knee, elbows, brow against the ice.

Note
Chapayev: a figure from the Russian Civil War who became a hero in
Soviet anecdotes.

★

Like a shattered embrasure,
it does not disturb the earth's peace,
like a wounded bird,
between the quiet and silence.

Limping, leaning,
on an uninjured wing,
I'll reach heaven's gates,
where evil is not welcome.

★

And He suffered, and for a moment
doubted – like ourselves.
That is, an incarnation of God,
neither notion, opinion,
idea, nor minds

add anything
or take anything away,
they defame themselves to the whole world
'the gods' will be amused,
only hear, 'Why do you lie!'

★

A rickety dog kennel,
threadbare forget-me-not,
alone, under the picket of the fence,
but we're happy with this.

And, behind the house,
at a slight distance,
a rumble, war not so close.
That pleases us, too.

★

It happened in August
all five sides lit up
to the strains of 'Mein lieber Augustin',
the Berlin military with its firm tread.

Muscovites sing 'The Apple' song,
Hungarians intone Liszt.
(Twenty years ago their capital, too,
was laid waste.)

Now it's the turn of the Bulgarians.
What suits their mood?
'Farewell Slavic girl'?
Ranks on the march,
Prague waking to the rumble of tanks.

★

Rien de rien

'No, nothing to regret.'
Neither the lost bag with the key in it,
the door permanently locked,
nor the scraps of a letter,
floating in the Dvina or the Svir.
Nor the summer lightning, the nocturnal birds
flying north in spring,
the unfinished dreams
settling into your server.

Note
The Dvina, the Svir: rivers in the north of Russia.

★

Enough to pass
four stops,
for the grass to be nipped by frost,
and words too.
Enough to exceed
the bounds of skill
for iambs to drop into the pit.

Besides, there's a sufficiency
of fumes in the street
to silence and
enfeeble the earth.

★

Who's forgotten and what?
And what's making someone feverish?
Next to the broken wash-basin
you yourself are seated, broken.

A sound scarcely begins before it dies down,
no beginning, no end,
a half-forgotten flame
illuminating half a face.

★

'…not awful to die'

    …but it is awful
to argue, hour by hour, with death,
to throw oneself onto the wedding pyre,
a viper nesting in the breast.

To look back in vain,
to the two, four, five, at the spots
of the past on the wall. Lovely
to torment oneself: 'Well, it wasn't for nothing?'

But angels easily take wing,
on the point of a needle,
the little bell-tower behind,
as a tear is carried off,
fighting for breath.

★

To I.R. Maximova, first listener to my 'Concerto for Orchestra'

> No castles, parks,
> mirrored halls,
> where a black-and-white Bartók
> summons a French horn,
>
> from Taganka to Solyanka
> running a signal:
> 'Time for a fight, or the dump,
> the dump, the du...'

Note
Taganka, Solyanka: Moscow streets.

★

Autobiographical

They gave the fool free rein, gave the rascal freedom,
And he beats his free head on a wall.

★

> And adding breath to the coal
> straighten up, repeat
> the primeval summons to flame:
> 'Burn, I tell you!'
>
> Burn bright,
> not in vain!
> Burn hot,
> no grief.

Burn, my star,
star of dawn,
illuminated,
within you
an incalculable heat,
while between us
only coldness,

the dark of cosmic ice
in a starry ocean.
Flame, star,
light my mist-shrouded bonfire!

★

Self-parody

1.
The Terek knocks
on the wild shore,
the tribesman knocks
on the wild shore.

Adjust to the fray
is all I have got to say.

2.
(on a set theme)

Once, an old woman had a little grey goat.
Eniki-beniki, ladushki-ladushki.

Granny was so fond of the little goat
(a he-goat, too), she was weak.

Grey wolves attacked the little white wolf,
like the Kama making its way into the Volga.

All that was left were two little horns and legs.
All the paths and roads overgrown.

Note
Eniki-beniki, ladushki-ladushki: an untranslatable refrain.

★

Like a virtual hand-drill into a virtual wall,
it stopped me sleeping all night.
Scarcely had I warmed my bones,
sleep creeping over me,
than they began to torture me.

This means, that what I sow
has long ago been reaped,
chasing crows from the ploughed field
and declining the Russian race,
through not all its cases,
in endless succession.

★

from Another 13 eight-liners

1.
A metro station,
named after a saint –
cannot be made out
which one.
The morning, like mineral water,
sparkling all the way down.
Never mind!
If only there were some honour.

4.
Socrates, you're a valorous man, but a lousy spouse,
your Xanthippe is slandered down the ages,
endlessly, undeservedly; furthermore,
her name is raised like a suffragette's

shield. So, that's why you took the hemlock
for the nineteenth and twentieth centuries of our era,
as the banqueting man at the end of his tether
says to Plato: 'For stuff like this, I'm dying?!'

★

Don't limp,
my trochees,
don't go lame,
or roll up,
like Boreas,
beginning to limp,
beyond April
and May,
lame,
limping,
like March,
like death.

Mile by mile,
I wander the universe,
pinning tails of untold loveliness
to mile-posts.

Is it you? – Yes, myself and you,
are in my selfish memory,
crawling into the bushes
with a cut vein.

Is it I? – It is, you, and I myself as well
withdrawing from non-being,
setting your image in my tattered memory,
not just to right it,
but also to understand,
transcending bounds,
rumpling, straightening, merging.

From *Poema bez poemy* [Poem without a Poem]
(2001)

Epigraph to the book *Last Poems of the Last Century*

Happy new century and a new breeze
over a hundred and one kilometres,
with the undeflected metre
of a sorrowful sheet.
One-two-three-four-five
a jack-rabbit began to jive,
while the wolf, lying low,
tried to crucify it.

★

Romance

The children of Lt. X
or the grand-kids of Capt. Y
didn't notice the mistake,
didn't notice that science had lost them,

that their locomotives
stuck in a marsh,
rusty, decaying, like scraps of flesh.
Why intone

those tunes? The willows
standing by themselves
make such a din.

The wheel in the marsh,
ravaged and rusty,
processions of power,
passing downhill.
That power, which gripped us by the throat
but didn't hold.

From nobody comes the question,
from nobody, a response.

★

Where it's not stamped down, measured
by the infantry or a passer-by,
there in clouds, before the people
of Euripidiope and Homerica

wage cosmic wars,
starry battalions on the move.
Cosmopolitans from Alitalia
Dante-faced, and tranquil,

cosmopolitans with Roman profiles,
squeeze the trigger fully,
and from the diasporas only spores remain.
Now, what had we lost, what wasted on booze,

won, or gained,
by pressure or persuasion,
what was totally deleted,
and what got stowed in the capsule?

The female sympathiser is certainly convivial,
a sweetie-pie, a pipelet, a receptacle of the spirit,
acceptably brittle,
like the first sleet underfoot
that year, when autumn lingered,
not a year passed,
but clouds were waking rustling,
and my soul scurrying over the snow.

If temples, cells and imperial chambers
are used for barns,
as we know, Messrs. Rousseau & Voltaire
are to blame.

Brave fellow,
we're not guilty at all,
that Rousseau was on his bell-tower
tugging at the great ropes,
or Voltaire setting fire
to ornate chambers.

Not guilty at all,
not a bit,
but let's repeat it,
or we may forget,
not in the least!

SELECTED POEMS

And correcting, improving,
still composing, in the back of the mind,
not a biography, but a life,
squeeze yourself into something firm
and stuff the gunpowder in while it's still dry,
light it, but take care not to burn yourself.

*

A poem without a poem,
a battle without a hero,
a trireme with no constellation is doomed

to navigate the ocean,
sailless and rudderless,
leaning over, squinting
as to whether there be any cry
from the sky: 'Land!'

Note
'A poem without a poem': a reference to Akhmatova's 'Poem without a Hero'.

*

Dear inky one,
pencil stub,
you and I are alarm clocks
from the clearance sale.

In the raspberry canes,
we are petty thieves.
Set your name down,
little one.

A final copy, or maybe just a draft
hot, or dewy,
violet,
but blue in the light.

★

What can I not forget,
subsiding, like a prisoner, in a corner?
I cannot remember but wouldn't lie to myself,
threading this needle.

This Ariadne's thread,
with which she sewed an entire labyrinth,
remove it! I don't wish to keep or preserve
this festering bandage.

These wounds, sores – where from?
Not to remember, not to forget either.
You lie in the bed you made, but the bed's
no place to grieve or love in.

★

A cup, a dish, a spoon…
Pour some weak tea.
You and I, at the table,
bother nobody.
After all, we're not in a zoo.

Spoon, cup, dishes…
Casting rods,
no hooks, just hangers.
To call someone and not to phone,
don't tease the beasts,
through the cage-bars.

Tea-urn…
But don't take it amiss,
put lump sugar in, too.
The spoon knocks against the glass,
don't sit there, like an idol,
made in haste.

★

Yesterday's terrifying ferment,
already forgotten?
Evil, peacefully dormant,
puffing gently?

Sleeps,
and dreams?
The rifle taken from the wall
still shoots straight.

★

With every passing day,
the earth is more visible.
On the horizon,
even the ocean
isn't cursed,
and seems drowsy,

lying here, my friend,
do you sniff
the lilac-scented air
in the unknown shadow land?
– To the Neva, and home!

Nothing more, nothing less,
a scrap of pain
and of patience,
a thorn of a prickly plant,
torn away, bare and scraping,
we put on the fire,
on the altar, not on itself...
I hang on the lever,
but how weighty the earth.

From *Chainaya roza* [Tea Rose]
(2002–5)

Between the roofs
smoke reaches for the sky;
between the ribs,
an extinct coal

still flutters
against the beaten sides,
with the heat of
a hard-winged beetle.

Neuralgia,
rib-nostalgia,
but if I lie,
I soar, like a beetle in the heat.

Between the roofs
and entrances to a tavern.
I'm no higher or lower
than a boot.

★

Against the glass pane, a knife,
like a knife against a pane of glass.
The glazier, seated in a corner
drinking tequila, not mineral water;

and, in a corner, between the glass stack
and a heap of sacks,
where stones burn down to ash,
like the progeny of gone times,

where even life has flown
like smoke in the beckoning dark.
Where death is mute, like poetry,
like a diamond, noiseless against a glass pane.

★

And former misfortune, they say,
doesn't matter; what does matter is metaphysics.
Forget, goose-foot, how you were plucked to the last leaf.
Forget the frozen ground,
those we buried not more than a metre deep.
The blue, golden endlessness,
eternity in reverse-perspective.

★

In the August sky, a flight of stars,
uncountable even by astrologers,
because the stars are discussing
the Creator and His work

the Creator and His humble creatures,
the Father and His prodigal offspring...
But the calendar pages turn,
December followed by January,
and only one star is forever
and saving us from the nets.

★

How, where, whence
did the rainbow extend itself
and shine, as if Fabergé himself
had suspended it...

★

... fell ... that behind which

In the pale, empty dark
you balance on scales,
behind the seventh curtain,
in the seventh heaven.

But the earth beneath
is both steppe-like and wooded,
spring arriving
over steppes, over woods.

Note: '... fell ... that behind which': an abbreviated version of lines by
Tatiana Kazanskaya used by Akhmatova as an epigraph to her *Seventh Book*:
'The seventh veil of mist fell, / that behind which spring appears'.

★

My mother was born in Russia
and died there,
four days after the demise
of the USSR.

But I was born in the Soviet Union
and shall probably die in France,
labelled 'Refugee, stateless,
a former Soviet citizen.'

★

from Military eight-liners

1.
Thanks to the hand, painstakingly tracing
an untidy signature, and date.
Thanks to the one playing hide-and-seek,
leaving a chink at least for the soldier,

when, battle-crazed,
he's rendered incapable,
but remembers his playground
and the rules of the game.

7.
What's happened to me,
in city P, this late spring?
I neither walk, drink, nor eat,
like a wise fool in city M.
Like some freak gazing out from a phial,
wondering whether the Achaean tanks
are on the move.
Time to open fire?
No, just a wooden horse!

8.
You'll say: everywhere,
spring is late.
No use smashing the crockery,
and going without sleep.

Another two plates?
No more weeping, or stammering:
Not guilty! Not my fault!
Don't put me on trial!

9.
And here's a Russian problem:
down or up the slope?
Amaryllis, even out of season,
sprouting again.

Two flowers on a single stem,
swigging,
like a drunken ache
in an empty boot, in a clearing.

11.
A review: how vague, the language,
the chaos of words and music,
an almost motionless melody
lurching back *à rebours*,
word-perception obliterated,
and logic – *à défaut*
(as though Comrade Friday had been commissioned
to review Defoe's book).

13.
One-two-three-four-five,
six-seven-eight.
And again, as in the past,
we're mowing the hay.

Mowing, carrying, and stooking it,
and not a drop to drink,
just the smoke
of burnt oakum.

★

What's he looking for,
like Jove in the rubbish dump?
What's he running from,
like the Wandering Jew?

Or the Eternal Ploughman,
knowing neither terror,
storm, nor blizzard.
Does the star on your brow

light your path
and dispose of terror?
Hurry, till you've
sown peace.

★

Yesterday, the evenings
were longer and brighter,
with a bee bustling
over pollen,

figuring out how to get
its scrap of honey,
flying over,
and then settling

on the quivering sage,
offering pollen,
as though Alcaeus
were warming to the metre.

★

from Square of discord

6.
Enter, and you will not get out,
step in,
sample, look around
at the Lord's blessings.

It was not He who created the Gulag,
but the twentieth century,
along with a man,
meaning myself and yourself.

From *Krugi po vode* [Circles in the Water]
(January 2006–August 2008)

I exit at the Gare de l'Est
taking leave of the Eastern frost,
I've said 'trans-sense language' makes no sense,
but try making it out,

like a moth among roses,
a smoothing-iron among crumpled day-dreams,
despite the heat and threats,
hearty mint-pills,

despite oneself… O, 'Trans-sense',
such green eyes, o clever cat!
Courage, don't leave the train,
on which you are travelling *gratis*.

★

What is it began to whisper
on a branch, at the window?
Didn't dare to twitter,
or, worse still, to whistle?
What, or who?

It's spring, the equinox,
winter, winter's term ended,
and it goes free, to the far,

furthest east,
and the further, the more dispiriting,
though spring makes for stumbling feet,

deletes snowdrift leftovers and
the remains of graves,
since resurrection is nearby,
at the exit-openings on white brows,

since God is love,
be ready for anything!

★

Neither stubs of tails, line-ends, full stops,
nor e-mails can rectify our handwriting.
And when you asked, 'How's the wife?' the word
sounds like 'strife', recalling the Zone
and you keep yourself like a freemason,
who was just a mason.
Not so much sleepy as sleepless.
Not sensitive, but disinclined to joke,
long sent to the devil and his mates.

Stamp the correspondence.
A true Russian will look like a crafty Pole,
dodging, lying, dissembling,
not even believing himself,
not trusting reflex or habit,
keys in the pocket, matches, lock-picks
for lovers beyond the river, and overseas
and past pleasure, in concert.

Placing a copyright notice on the correspondence,
you yourself are on the list,
alphabetical, where ears, hands, feet
walk in pairs behind, on the road,

like a convict with his escort, liver
and spleen together,
and everyone clothed in thin skin,
which might tear any moment
to leave you naked, naked, friends!

The correspondence in the corresponding whistling of birdlife,
no grand design (i.e. no greatness),
no intention (i.e. no undermining or overthrowing),
no intent (i.e. no escaping encirclement),
no thoughts, however limp and unthreatening,
just rhymes in twos or threes.

★

Don't restrain yourself! Out with the truth!
as punctiliously as in the old days,
and remember that Russia's favourite pastime
is laying folks on altars.

★

Lord, hear me,
I'm not just part of the crowd.
                    — I hear, child!
I'm not asking you to substitute
the twitching thread of
my destiny.

Give whatever you want,
as you gave me a pencil and notebook.
Better listen to me, Lord,
so I don't get confused.

No road worker can set Raspail
right. The dry sun melts
this impotent Babylon.
As in childhood, I chew pitch
till my teeth clog,
till an inaudible bell
resounds in my ears.

Climbing Parnassus,
I bronze like a nymph,
yesterday's sister
to the squandered heavens.
'Have mercy on us, wretched sinners',
I whisper, and stumble,
at once waking
(a dream dreamt this morning).

Note
'Raspail', transliterated, suggests an unfinished road, hence the reference
to 'road-worker'. The action of the dream takes place near the intersection
of the Boulevards Raspail and Montparnasse in Paris.

★

Who is knocking at the brow, but from without,
my hermetic skull breaks,
through the cracking, deeper and duller,
a weighty ferry-boat knocking on the shore
and drifting off, over and over,
sleeping or awake, awake, or dreaming,
leaving the home shore,
heading straight for the bottom, under a green flame.

Do you, do we, do I know, who's there
tapping Morse on my frontal bone?
The delineated route, the unattained heights,
like honey flowing, towards postal headquarters
and, with summer, the century, and riverwards
like a flow of milk, towards submarine lawns,
mortal sins and forgiven trespasses,
to the point where you'll be forever free.

★

Logs in the oven don't burn, but do warm,
don't dissolve, fall apart, fly up the chimney,
don't possess loads of time,
drinking and feeding from the name of the udder.

Wonderful are little logs and lumps,
a wondrous miracle, without smoke or fumes,
creating and burning patiently, cheerfully,
like an untended garden fence.

★

Wherever you went –
by crooked street
or winding path –
whatever was found
went up in smoke,
you won't bring home.

Whatever you sang,
a song of triumph,
or lament for fallen rebels,
the rooster flew off,
mould got a grip
on the unfinished lines of verse.

Whatever flowed,
rhymeless, on the off-chance
whatever sounded from the loudspeakers
this smoke, ash,
these lines on the bonfires,
begin the fairy-tale at the start.

★

I shall rake up on the wind, like a candle,
lose all, warmth and light,
but not lie, even in the heat of the moment,
when you ask: Yes or No?

I'll bury my brow, like a snowball,
in the cold, snowy, nocturnal dark,
when you draw a knife across the glass
and hide in the corner, defeated,

between oven and dresser.

★

Snack on some medication,
don't sing, smoke, or breathe.
The non-diminished power of the state
over the poor soul's physique,

and the metaphysical tremor
is especially strong and sacred
where they box the soul's ears
but don't subject the flesh to execution.

★

from KRUGI PO VODE

By this overgrown route,
this narrow,
half-trodden path,
with a half-whispered song,

a half-smile, half-tear,
suspended from an eyelash,
you walk to school, till the end of life
learning words, verbs,
how to decline them, that is,
join, not giving in.

★

These waves, hillocks,
these little corpuscles on the parquet,
tears and snivels,
whether guffawing, or wailing,
I take at face value,

trusting those who are
as weak as me, and as sinful,
since the One who is King and Queen,
in Whom I live, without becoming brutalised,
is consoled by this trifle.

★

And Troy has not fallen

To Olga Martynova and Oleg Yuriev

And Troy will not fall, but will stand forever,
as long as a single poet survives
in this moonlit world. Even if half-alive.
A half-poet. The reader, who is non-mendacious.
While the *aoidos* his hexameters murmurs.
While Hades is no place for our misfortunes,
our torments, while the blizzard
is not blowing hither and thither
the torn-out pages of books,
while the Hippocrene's spring is flowing
even from the aridity of our emaciated souls.
Even from a puddle, from shallow, frozen
pools. King Priam's house does not
freeze, even when iced over.

Note
'As long as a single poet survives': a reference to Pushkin's poem 'Exegi monumentum'.

★

What is relevant — age, weight,
a French metre or a Russian pound?
But these what-ifs and ifs,
this patience and hard work,
and these thoughts, mice in an armchair...
And you'll throw yourself into a pond,
and a psaltery from an old song
will wear down into ballast and gravel.

★

For the first time I feel sorry for the unwritten poems.
The head was full not of these, or those, but of life –
a search for living quarters and stuffed packages,
weeping over keys and over broken glass

on Yasik's engraving, over the church, round the corner,
whether this be a turning point in my life or broken,
or simply that a nobody came to spend the night
on the squat Japanese couch?

Note
Yasik: the artist Yaroslav Gorbanevsky, Natalya Gorbanevskaya's son.

★

Malakoff

In the steppes is a burial mound.
Anika the Warrior lies lifeless.

Malakh, for whom a burial mound,
of course, would also be lifeless,
at that moment was not given
to the enemy in profanation,

but was decently buried,
as in the medieval world
the tribes still managed,
for their military.

But many years after
the enemy threatened the *kurgan*
and their own, not our three-coloured banner,
they set on the heights.

And the enemy fly into a rage, their faces reddening;
clapping, shaking their hands,
and since then, this wretched Paris suburb
has been called Malakhovka.

Notes

Malakhov Kurgan was strategically important high ground south-east of
Sevastopol. Named after Captain M.M. Malakhov, who lived there from
1827 to 1836, it was famously defended by the Russian forces against the
Anglo-French troops during the Crimean War in 1854–55, and again in
1942 against the Nazis. Malakhovka: the name of both a Moscow suburb
and a Paris suburb.

★

Unbearable is a poem's eruption.
Something broke the net,
and the fish is slithering to freedom.
Whether I strip a trap, a chain, or a necklace,
I dare to be bold.
A stagnating lump dissolves in my throat.

★

I go, go, don't whistle,
I'd like to, but don't know how.
Very soon I'll fly
to 'where the sky is bluest'.

And again, not whistling,
unrolling the scroll,
not reading it, not rising
over the useless attempts.

An aeroplane,
whether I'll get to my destination,
where the non-eternal ice of a tin whistle
turns into flowing honey.

★

I know, know,
hear, hear:
a horse's frisky head
has insinuated itself on the roof.

I travel, travel
an open field,
I shall come to you, brother,
around summer, in a week.

the little horse tosses
its head
and prances over the cut grass,
like a grasshopper.

★

> *All I have is a voice…*
> W.H. Auden

These places
where I've never been,
cold of a canvas
on the flanges of paradise.
Notes from a page
playing improbably,
you look through the window;
boringly, comically.

There in September
you have passed, in a wagon,
in the flaming heat,
having omitted to find
lodging for the night,
and, at dawn,
finding yourself in flight,
taking a bow,
pulling out the hook.

Dawn is coming
from the East,
with six ammunition-wagons
sixty eyes,
so, the violin stopped
not for nothing
singing before its time
floorboards creaking.

★

Is there nothing to read?
The bookshelves are heavy with books.
They look like insatiable wolves:
who'll gobble up whom?

It's understood that
I'll be swallowed
and will play the part
of lupine satiety, not in my dream.

They'll come down,
bury me under themselves,
and there's no gun,
no hunter,

to unstitch the belly
and extricate my remains.
The Lord lit an icon-lamp,
but it went out.

2006–8

★

Sometimes silence is like music,
speech like noise.
But that stream, in its narrow ravine
burbles in a trans-sense language,

what is the main thing, inexpressible,
not to be expressed in words
or notes. And pre-winter is,
like hoarfrost between you and me.

★

Three poems about the rain

1.
But do you like
the wind and the rain?
Without an umbrella
do you fondle by lips?

You suck the exoticism
into your lungs,
the buoyant foliage
of different kinds of willows,

they totter,
they sway,
and breathe facelessly,
weeping endlessly.

2.
Close the gate,
don't open it,
don't let
the dry thread go.

Don't let
gift or debt
shrink. You'll go
to Kushka
and Aristan,

swallow countless
celestial tears
and unanswered
earthly threats.

Threats, tears,
armfuls of roses,
rain, storms –
that's the question.

3.
Only three? Three thousand
in future, and past!
Already dreams of a candle
have been realised, of those tender,

flowing contacts, that douse heat
and quench thirst...
The cloud-master has unclenched his fist,
and I'll suffer no more.

Notes
Kushka: a city in Turkmenia and the most southerly point in the former
USSR. Aristan: a fabled city in a children's song.

★

Somewhere, someone,
undefined.
Why do you look at me, askance,
in amazement?

A young man, a girl,
nothing to be amazed at,
nothing to look askance at,
forelock, pigtail.

You're young, young,
strings ringing in your heads,
blueing in your eyes.
Heron is sickly, stricken,
– No, no, it hasn't died.
The poet has withered away.

But music and in the deaf ear
it sounds dull.
Scent can be smelted
and a good spirit is silent.

As you listen,
listening carefully,
not because there are ears,
but because... No,
without any 'because',
'since' or 'therefore'.
Like a cat hunting a mouse,
sounds catching the light.

★

Walk without hurrying
down the leisurely little path,
mend the broken link,
not with lace, but darning.

And whomever you approach
and meet on the way –
fly slowly, gently,
like a breeze, not the wind.

★

from KRUGI PO VODE

Like a shop assistant opening the store,
I open my computer in the morning,
I twitch my ears and an eyeless white mouse,
move my lips, in my modest way,
like a Latinist priest, intoning the mass.

Like Comrade Stalin, I grasp linguistics,
to preserve, to decode, to send out – I know it all,
but suddenly the unknown chains fall away
and I'm sitting and toiling over the month of May.

Note
'I grasp linguistics': a reference to a popular prison song, 'Comrade Stalin,
you are a great scholar, you grasped linguistics', written by Yuz
Aleshkovsky in 1959.

★

Two poems about something or other

1.
Of course, it's not yet
the real autumn.
Bloodhounds sniff about, searching for
my near-obliterated footsteps.
But already it's not so warm,
the heat not so intense.
To raise it – and shoot from there,
and a funeral wreath.

Sweeping the first fall of leaves
with my cloak,
with a four-pronged rake,
again I step on the edge,
and, in the penultimate ray,
wanting to share with you
my mellifluous betrayal,
I'll fuse into sheer truth.

2.
The naked truth,
or a deliberate lie,
to be read as quickly as possible,
or you'll not make it out,

or leading into atonality
some melody,
not to squelch the modicum
of April rain,

or, having atomised the attack,
you'll shake your shaggy locks
and, barely alive,
break into sob.

And the sobs will resound,
not what you expected, not that.
And exile, banishment will resound
but somewhere else, not there.

★

Search and you'll find,
I walk, prodding with my cane,
joints creaking,
cracking, ticking,

like a clock. One more hour,
to traverse the little wood,
the orchard, the swamp,
like a horse or a lizard –
all the same, something will turn up,
appear, be found.

⋆

Even so, into a noose, into heaven,
or the old-world horde,
we're not proud, not secure,
not slaves, or lords,
dying in the old way.

Praying, as in the old days,
at the threshold of the way,
into blizzards, cover the confusion,
fainting fits, slowness,
commotion, murk, filth.

Having crossed the threshold,
I'll embrace darkness and the rain-clouds,
the smoke of the abyss,
where lion lies down with lamb
in an ambush of accord.

⋆

How few pinball machines now in Paris,
what's more, no smoking in cafés,
you screw up your eyes, like a half corpse,
insufficiently cooled.

Landscape, landscape – in truth, a landscape,
the more appealing, the more wretched,
rainy, like a birch tree on the edge of a grave.
What would you give for it?

From *Razvilki* [Forks in the Road]
(August 2008–December 2009)

Not trying to surprise,
not in the least,
I tugged this thread
from youth to old age.

The thread, not to be mended,
if it gets broken.
The passion, not to be harnessed
to grief or joy.

The thread, stretching
into the cooling night.
I gaze, like a drunk,
at the diminishing ball of thread.

★

Deaf and old,
I fly to my rest.
Apart from tea and coffee,
beholden to no one
for anything.

Little springs running down slopes,
freshly green in March,
I hear, hear
the soft, gentle sound
of their sources, their sinuosities,
and draw the bow-string
of my rhyme.

★

In general I don't fear rain,
but when I go out, in my sandals,
and it's raining
I know I'll catch cold
and will cough badly,
as, probably, the syphilitic leader once coughed.

This sickening simile
torments me in nightmares,
I give my scout's-word
not to go out
when it's raining,
to wear my sandals.

Note
'The syphilitic leader' is Lenin.

★

I live modestly, but quite well,
don't plough the field,
don't waste my time,
as on a garden plot,
I treasure my work, not under any jurisdiction,

and I am indifferent to other people's views,
knowing no fear which shakes the earth
under stormy northern lights,
summoning, but unalive.

From *Shtoito. Stikhi 2010* [Sumthing. Poems 2010]
(2010)

I loved freedom,
neither stole, nor robbed,
just broke a cup
on the general's head.

And now I languish behind bars,
like a caged bird.
'Let's fly, friend!', comes the whisper.
'Can you?'

★

Verbs pursue me,
non-substantive, bare,
follow me closely,
banging, bruising my elbows,
slamming the door behind,
mounting the clouds.

They hurry, stand in each other's way
and console one another:
'Let's take a breather.
This hit will make me dark,
and how are we to keep pace with her,
although following very close.'

I pity them and release them, poor things,
losing heart:
'Tie me up, conjugate me!'
I tighten my belt,
and harness the familiar team,
lifting my head.

The Language Problem of a Poet in Exile

Address by Natalya Gorbanevskaya to the full editorial board
meeting of *Kontinent*, Munich, May 1983

In one of the Orthodox services of the week before Easter, there is
the utterance: 'Give me a Word, the Word'; the Mother of God is
addressing Christ. Detaching these words from their liturgical
context, we still keep repeating them. Even silently, we exclaim:
'Word, give me a word!'

Joseph Brodsky was right when he remarked that it was not, as
we imagined, language that is the poet's instrument but the poet
who is the instrument of language. The whole question is whether
language will consent to be used, not seizing up, not growing blunt,
especially when subjected to new influences, unfamiliar conditions.
In my view, the unfamiliar new conditions may not only renew the
instrument and give it a new lustre, but will adjust it, enabling it to
perform tasks for which it was not designed. I am speaking about
the conditions experienced by the poet in exile.

Leaving the Soviet Union, we lose nothing, and we gain the
desired freedom, entirely unconnected with the quality of our
poetry. Freedom gives us the means of publishing widely and not
being incarcerated on that account.

Leaving Russia, on the other hand, we lose a lot. We lose our
connection with a habitual circle of readers; though in the end we
find new ones here, and establish a new type of relationship with
the previous readers, more elevated, based, perhaps, on the pure
relationship of poem to reader.

We lose our native landscape, one way or another assimilated into
the alphabet of our poetry, but, like previous generations of exiles,
carry the dust of our roads and the melted asphalt of our city
pavements on the soles of our shoes. However, if, besides the

external, we are given an internal view of what is not visible to us here, we see things afar more clearly, and what we see is transformed by exposure to the Russian language.

We lose our linguistic milieu – or more accurately a linguistic element far more significant than casual conversation in the relatively narrow émigré circles, surrounding us in the street, in the endless queues, in the packed trams or metros. This frightens us most – crossing the frontier, we cross, as it were, into an airless space. And, at first, this fear – I think it is fear, not the loss itself – creates undoubted difficulties.

For me, and, as I've observed, for other Russian poets of the new emigration, the first months of life in the West are a period of bewilderment. It is as if the poet did not know what to do with himself, whether to fall silent for a while, or to write – at least that's what I felt – settling inertly into a former *modus operandi*.

If we do not know the language of the country in which we reside, it irritates us that, around us in the metro, in the street, in cafés, everybody is speaking an indistinguishable babble. If we know the language, instead of an indistinguishable noise, fragments of conversations, radio and TV news, commentaries, film dialogue enter the ears. It is still incomprehensible; why should I need it? The fear of a vacuum becomes justified.

In the medley of senselessness, in a foreign language, even small children speaking it, even if not distinctly or meaningfully – at first the words are indistinct, which we ought at first to hear and only afterwards note down. From this noise, either we grow deaf, or on the contrary, the ear, trying to distinguish between sounds, grows more acute and begins to hear turns of phrase, subtleties, sophisticated allusions as never before. Truth to tell, I think that only that ear is deaf, which did not listen attentively before.

This picture, of which I have observed several examples, shows that beyond the period of loss, silence, inert poetry, there is an acute elevation of standards. This is explained, in my view, by the fact that the collision with an alien linguistic element provokes a conscious, active relationship in the search for words. By consciousness I do not mean naked rationalism or cold calculation. It is simply that earlier on we caught poems in traps laid for them, like hares that had infiltrated our allotments, but now we are entering known and unknown hunting terrains and catching all kinds of known and unknown game – including those same hares, wild goats, boars, unicorns.

The foreign language shocks, at first. Hardly managing to assimilate several words in French, I wrote: 'What a language! It doesn't distinguish between whether one has travelled by vehicle or on foot.' Like English and Italian, French does not distinguish between travel on foot and travel by conveyance; in the Slavic head this is incomprehensible. Whether we know the language well or not, we relate it to our own language and translate both ways. We make an attempt to combine two languages, imposing one on the other, and treating our own language as a foreign one, dictionary-based, as the means of expression and reflection – language as an instrument. But relating to it as an instrument, we stop it fully using us *as* its instrument.

It is hard for me to explain when and how the moment came when the elements of the two languages stopped being the right side and the wrong side, mutual translation, and became sharply distinct, but I know that such a moment does arrive for a poet. For that reason, knowledge of foreign languages, for a poet, presents no danger, as it does for a prose writer, and even more so for an émigré journalist; in addition to which, the daily and even professional needs of prose writers are often harmful to it, spoiling the language. Curious observation (I cannot give precise figures, but can vouch for the validity of what I am saying): fewer than half of the Russian prose-writers and more than half of the Russian poets living in America, and especially in Europe, speak the language of the country in which they reside. And it is not a matter of prose writers being more lazy, or less capable. The prose writer instinctively, as a self-defence mechanism, detaches himself from the foreign language, since the language of prose is more liable to be eroded by foreign elements; the language of prose depends more on what is within the author than on what is above him – more on what is being spoken around him on a daily basis.

I do not write prose fiction, but translate both prose fiction and social and political writings. I write a good deal of literary criticism and political surveys, but however much I try to control it, I am always using Gallicisms and Polonisms. I am convinced, however, that this does not affect my poetry. If one encounters in the poetry foreign words, turns of phrase, speech, they are always underlined, marked off as intentional devices. This very language, my Russian poetical language, is using me as its instrument, using one particular feature – my knowledge of a foreign language. I speak about myself because I know myself directly, more than I know others, my experience, however, being far from unique.

Possibly, Western participants in our meeting consider that having decided to discuss the language problems of a poet in exile, I should speak about how difficult it is for us poets to write, and perhaps suggest some means of ameliorating the situation. My conclusions are as follows: the linguistic problems of the poet in exile are not so arduous as are the daily problems of life for ordinary émigrés. Moreover, the poet, like no one else, receives support from his own language and can take refuge in it. And even the fact of discussing our language problems, the eternal obstacles and negotiations with the language – this very fact lends our poetry its particular distinction, or, as they say in the West, a new quality.

I think that, insofar as we do not forget that poetry is not an innate gift but comes from above, we can deal with any linguistic problem that arises.

Interview with Natalya Gorbanevskaya
by Valentina Polukhina

VP: *This is our third conversation. The first two were about Joseph Brodsky, but now I should like to talk about you and about your poetry. When did you begin to write poetry?*

NG: I composed my first poems at the age of five. These are nothing like those which Kornei Chukovsky described in his book *From Two to Five*. Their poetics is similar to that of my poetry in later years. I can give you an example:

> My soul was simmering
> whilst I was making the broth.
> My Ludmila was asleep
> and there weren't enough groats.

Generally speaking, I think the same principle governs my writing even now; in school, aged twelve, I started putting much effort into writing graceless verses in the Young Pioneer/Komsomol/Soviet mode. Later, at the university, I wrote and wrote, and the ball started rolling. I have preserved only the poems written since 1956. I suppose I started writing only in 1956, when I was twenty.

VP: *In 1953, you enrolled as a student of Moscow State University. Why were you twice expelled?*

NG: The first time was nonsense, I myself to blame. My so-called fame came from a faculty paper, which published a critical article on me and a few other first- and second-year students, accusing us of being followers of a decadent tendency. This contributed to my expulsion. Also, I didn't have a grade in Physical Training and the faculty chair told me I wouldn't be allowed to take the exams and would be expelled. So, I myself quit before that could happen. The second time was more serious. The formal grounds for expulsion were on account of my missing classes, but I missed only those I'd already taken. In reality, I was expelled after the trial of two friends, having been called as a witness, as it turned out the only defence witness. Everyone connected to the trial was expelled under one pretext or another.

VP: *The year 1956 is known as that of the suppression of the Hungarian Uprising, altering the consciousness of a whole generation, hence the designation 'the generation of 1956'. Was this re-evaluation of Soviet values reflected in your poetry? Am I correct in reading your poem 'And the fire in the stove went out' as a response to the events in Hungary?*

NG: Not just that one. All three poems of 1956 which begin any of my collections are connected to Hungary and to what happened in the USSR itself.

VP: *Who and what formed your poetic taste?*

NG: When I was eleven, I read and loved Blok (now I don't like his work); then it was Mayakovsky (now, I don't like him at all, not even the early verse). But my infatuation with his work led the way: at fifteen, when I was already in the ninth grade, I used to go to the Mayakovsky Museum and Library and read a lot. Mayakovsky led me to Khlebnikov. But my real aesthetic education began when I got to know Krasovitsky, Chertkov and Khromov, especially the first two. Via Krasovitsky's poems, I came to Pasternak (his poems were far easier after reading Krasovitsky). The same poets gave me insight into Zabolotsky's *Scrolls* (*Stolbtsy*). I copied by hand both *Scrolls* and Pasternak's *Second Birth* (*Vtoroe Rozhdenie*). I didn't even dream, at the time, of possessing a typewriter. Chertkov gave me a volume of *Unpublished Khlebnikov*. His library contained practically everything and I read and kept on reading.

VP: *Why did you reject all your poems written before 1962?*

NG: Not all, but most. I kept the best. So, when I visited Akhmatova, I brought her only poems I was not ashamed of. And even later, I discarded a few poems, but not as many as before.

VP: *You got to know Akhmatova in 1962. Please tell me about your meetings with her.*

NG: In June 1961, Dmitry Bobyshev took me to Komarovo, but when we arrived it turned out that Akhmatova was in Moscow. At the time I was a correspondence student at Leningrad University, and twice a year I had to go to Leningrad for exams. During the winter of 1961–62, I didn't go to Leningrad because I had given birth to my son. One day I went to the editorial offices of *Litera-turnaya Gazeta*, where my close friend Valentin Nepomnyashchy worked, and I told him I was going to Leningrad and wanted to be introduced to Akhmatova. However, Galina Kornilova told me that Akhmatova was in Moscow and that I should go and see her. I declined, feeling it would be an imposition. Galina said: 'Here's the phone. Call her!' So, in great embarrassment, I called, and Akhmatova asked me over the next day. I went to Ordynka Street where she was staying with the Ardov family. It was good I hadn't visited her a year earlier, because at the time my poems weren't much good, though I wrote a lot. Later I discarded most of them.

And then, in spring 1962, I managed to write some poems, including two of my so-called classics, like 'A Soldier in the Andersen Army' and 'Concerto for Orchestra'. Anna Andreevna liked them and told me so, as she might have told anyone, so as not to offend. But the next day Kornilova rang and said Anna Andreevna had told her she would soon be in Komarovo and invited me to see her.

And so I come to Leningrad, to the University, and meet someone who tells me it is rumoured Akhmatova liked my poems a lot. My fame, it seems, had preceded me.

One fine December day, in 1962, visiting Akhmatova, I was allowed to copy her *Requiem*. This cycle of poems was written in 1935–40, during the Stalin Terror. For many years, only select friends of the poet had heard them. Even Akhmatova herself and her numerous readers never committed *Requiem* to paper. But then *Novy Mir* published *One Day in the Life of Ivan Denisovich*, and

Akhmatova thought, perhaps, that the time had come for *Requiem* too.

Handing me a pen, Anna Andreevna said: 'Solzhenitsyn copied *Requiem* with the pen you are now holding.' After Akhmatova's death, on the day of my arrest, 24 December 1969, this copy, with the title page which Akhmatova herself wrote, was confiscated in the search.

Coming home from Akhmatova, I at once copied *Requiem* on all the typewriters available to me (I didn't yet have one of my own). My two dozen copies soon grew to a hundred. In May 1963, in Leningrad, I gave a typewritten copy to Andrzej Drawicz. That year, in the West, a pale booklet, *Requiem*, was published in the review *Twórczosc* in Polish translation. In 1967 I had the opportunity to recite excerpts from *Requiem* in public, at the Polytechnic Museum.

I saw Akhmatova regularly from May 1962 till January 1966 – the last time being in the Botkin Hospital. She certainly liked me, I can vouch for that. As for me, each time I saw her, it was like receiving an undeserved medal. But that's not the main thing. The main thing was that knowing her, I became a real person.

VP: *You know Polish well and have translated some Polish poets, including Czesław Miłosz. When and why did you study Polish? What benefit did knowledge of the language bring you in the 50s?*

NG: At the end of the 50s, in the first half of 1960, the Polish language was above all a 'window on Europe'; it was in Polish that we could read Kafka, Faulkner and other European and American writers, still unpublished in Russian. I became deeply interested in Polish literature and history almost at once.

I think the influence came partly through Polish films, which by chance I was able to sample at the time of the youth festival in 1957; *The Attempt* and *Ashes and Diamonds* were shown in Russia in 1965; a year after I read Andrzejewsky's novel and began really to read in Polish.

VP: *In April 1968, you were the first editor of the* samizdat *publication* A Chronicle of Current Events. *How was it compiled and what was the purpose of this journal?*

NG: The stimulus was the abundance of information in *samizdat* about the political trials – Alexander Ginsburg's book about the Sinyavsky trial (1966); Litvinov on the trials of Khaustov and Bukovsky; a vast number of protest letters after Galanskov and Ginsburg were sentenced to a term in the camps, and especially Anatoly Marchenko's book, *My Testimony*; also what we knew of the political camp regime; documents on the persecution of Christians and others. Nobody was collecting this information, since we were all busy. As it happens, I was in the last stages of pregnancy and on leave. So, I had free time. I consulted friends (Ilya Gabai, Pavel Litvinov, Yuly Kim and Irina Yakir) and received their blessing. I set to work.

With the first issue, I was working almost on my own. Only a few people knew what I was up to. I opened the first number with an account of the Ginsburg/Galanskov trial. After this inaugural *samizdat* issue, it became easier to collect information. People who knew we were bringing out the *Chronicle* passed on the information they had. Thanks to good relations with the families of political prisoners, information became more plentiful. So, for the 1968 issue, I compiled a survey of *samizdat* publications for that year. Subsequently, 'Samizdat News' became a regular feature of the journal.

The *Chronicle*, as with all other *samizdat* publications, was retyped by its small readership. Western radio stations mentioned it, and Radio Liberty broadcast its entire contents. It was a good decision to publish the *Chronicle* without naming the editors. This enabled it to continue for over fifteen years, with changes of editors, some of them imprisoned, other exiled, but without changes in its essential nature.

The *Chronicle* was modelled on the *Ukrainian Bulletin* of the *Chronicle of the Catholic Church of Lithuania*. The editors of the Helsinki Group relied on the experience of the *Chronicle*, as did the working groups against the use of psychiatry for political purposes. By remaining thematically a general journal, reporting on the whole country, the *Chronicle* preserved its unique position.

VP: *Tell us how, on 25 August 1968, you participated in the demonstration in Red Square against the Soviet intervention in Czecho-slovakia.*

NG: On 21 August, the very day that the intervention in Czechoslovakia occurred, Anatoly Marchenko was being tried in Moscow. The pretext for the trial was infringement of passport regulations; the real reason, of course, being his book, *My Testimony*, the first detailed, first-hand account of the political prison camps under Khrushchev and Brezhnev, as well as of the protest movement against the anti–Czech Soviet press campaign. All my friends intended to show up at the court (knowing from experience that they wouldn't be admitted). I alone had to stay at home to breastfeed my baby.

I was wondering what to do. To demonstrate seemed the only sensible thing. By nature I am not keen on this kind of protest, preferring to sit in front of a typewriter and contribute to *samizdat*, editing letters, or work on the *Chronicle*. But suddenly I realised that I could no longer limit myself in that way. My friends felt the same way, turning up at the courthouse. All they had to do was to agree on a time and place. Larisa Bogoraz told me where and when it was to be: Red Square, around noon, at the Place of Execution opposite the Historical Museum. So that there should be no mistake, we would sit on the wall surrounding the Place of Execution.

I made the posters early in the morning of the 25th, sewed them together and stuck them on poles. One was in Czech, 'Long live a free and independent Czechoslovakia'; the other was the rallying call of the Polish rebels, 'For your freedom and ours'. In a few minutes four posters were shown. People began to gather round us, while from the far corners of the square, ahead of the crowd, came those whose purpose was to put an end to this demonstration. They rushed across and tore up the posters, not even glancing at what was written on them. A man and a woman with briefcases and a heavy sack began beating Pavel Litvinov. I turned round and saw Fainberg being beaten. I heard two comments: 'They're all Jews!' 'Thrash the anti-Soviets!'

In a few minutes the first car arrived. They picked up the guys and piled them in. I was on my own. The infant was woken by the noise, but stayed quiet. 'Get going, girl! someone kept saying. I stayed put. I thought, if they don't take me, I'll stay here till 1 pm and then leave. But then a man and that same woman who had been beating Pavel with a bag came through the crowd. He grabbed my arms — the woman near me just about managed to hand me the infant. They shoved me into a car. I got to the window and shouted 'Long live a free Czechoslovakia!' As I was shouting this, the woman hit me violently on the mouth. I opened the window again and managed to shout: 'We're being taken to the 50th division of the militia', but, again, she hit me on the mouth. It was humiliating and painful. 'How dare you hit me!' I shouted both times. And both times she muttered: 'Who's hitting you? No one's hitting you.'

VP: *Clearly you behaved heroically. What made you engage in this dangerous activity?*

NG: We were not heroes and not crazy, simply people determined to obey their conscience. The 25th August demonstration was not an act in the political struggle, it was ethical. The participation of each of us individually was based on an ethical passion, on a feeling of personal responsibility for our country's history.

The Warsaw Pact intervention was called an act of 'fraternal support', and the entire Soviet press was filled with declarations of national support for it. So, if even a single individual did not approve, this 'fraternal support' would cease to be national. But to make this clear we had to be open about it. The purpose was to distance ourselves from the 'approval of all people', or – to put it crudely – to keep a clean conscience.

VP: *Why were you not arrested with the other demonstrators?*

NG: I had my three-month-old son with me and so was not taken right away. We were all interrogated and searched at the 50th division of the militia, near Pushkin Square. The search started at 10 pm and lasted till 2 am. There were four of us (my mother, myself, and my two children) in a single room of a communal apartment. When they were leaving, they said to me 'You have your children to thank that the search was over so quickly.' I did not expect them to leave me at home; I thought they'd throw me in gaol.

I decided that if I remained at liberty, I would have to see this through – write a letter on the reason for the demonstration, its purpose, its placards and its participants, to prevent idle gossip. I wrote and dispatched this letter on 28th August. With the help of Andrey Amalrik, who had connections with foreign correspondents, the letter was conveyed to the chief editors of *Rude Pravo*, *Unita*, the *Morning Star*, *Humanité*, *The Times*, *Le Monde*, the *Washington Post*, the *Neue Zürcher Zeitung* and the *New York Times*.

VP: *Your arrest in 1969 and compulsory treatment in the Kazan psychiatric prison is reflected only in passing in your poems. Why were you so restrained.*

NG: Because it's a 'black hole'. Because I commented on it for ten years in different countries, especially France (in an effort to draw attention to those who were in the same position; I didn't speak about it before my emigration). At a conference in Paris, I said that if compulsory treatment was torture, then to talk about it during these ten years had become another form of torture for me, and this is the last time I am speaking about it.

VP: *What did you learn about man and humanity as a result of your arrests and confinement to a prison psychiatric hospital?*

NG: I think I learnt no more than one can learn from literature. I must say that in the Butyrskaya prison Dostoyevsky and Dickens were the best reading. I learnt that in any of Dickens's novels, you'll find either a prison, a workhouse or a trial. Even, it seems, in the cheerful pages of *The Pickwick Papers*!

VP: *You were baptised in 1967. Did your faith help you endure the ordeal of the psychiatric prison?*

NG: Hard to say. It helped a bit. On the other hand, one had to hide one's faith or it would be treated as just another 'symptom'.

VP: *Politics, which has played such a large part in your life, has been secondary in your poetry. Is this displacement of politics to the periphery a conscious one?*

NG: Politics never occupied any place in my life. What is called political is simply civil, i.e. to do with personal behaviour. So it is as personal as the poetry.

VP: *You were released in February 1972. How have you lived and supported yourself until your emigration in December 1975?*

NG: I translated and wrote essays. I have always worked on a temporary basis, or in some bibliographical capacity.

VP: *In 1973 you accused yourself: 'I did not save Warsaw then or Prague later / It was I, it was I, and my guilt cannot be expiated'. You felt guilty for the actions of the Soviet communists.*

NG: Not for the actions of Soviet communists, but for myself. Don't tell me that historical and national guilt does not exist, but only the responsibility of each for what he or she has done. My response is that no one should avoid historical guilt as an individual, but if the individual feels it, he takes it upon himself, it is his emotion or his right. So, I wrote: 'I did not save Warsaw then or Prague after'. Warsaw in 1944, Prague in 1968. For a long time I wanted to write poems about the Warsaw uprising, beginning with the line '... and the army halted on the other bank', but I didn't. Perhaps it was too direct, too factual. 'I did not save...' is not factual. At the time of the Warsaw uprising, I was eight years old. Not factual, but having to do with some deep reality, a sense of responsibility for what my nation has perpetrated, and a response. Neither in 1939 nor in 1940, the year of the Katyn massacre, nor in 1944, of course, could I personally have been held responsible for what was done by the parties and governments, yet the sense of guilt is not the subject of a judicial inquiry and does not make such demands. This is perhaps at the root of 'my Poland'.

VP: *Did you know that after the publication of the English collection of your poems in 1972, the agent of Jane Fonda phoned your translator Daniel Weissbort and expressed the actress's wish to play you on the screen?*

NG: No, I didn't know, but it's comical. She is two heads taller than me. Most likely, she wanted to play a heroine.

VP: *Over a quarter of a century has passed since 1976 when you came to France. How did you come to live in Paris?*

NG: Of course I didn't flee somewhere, I fled *from* somewhere.

Where I was to go from Vienna, I'd no idea. But Vladimir Maksimov, in the name of the Montgeron Fund, invited me and so I went to Paris. It was the right place for me, both in the sense of work, fruitful years on *Kontinent* and *Russkaya mysl*, and in the sense of the feel of the city, which became mine, and I its. I am a Parisian. And at the same time I remain a Muscovite. I still feel that way.

VP: *Has prolonged exposure to the French language had an effect on your Russian?*

NG: If so, it has to do with enrichment, greater flexibility. I spoke of this in a presentation on 'The Language Problem of a Poet in Exile'. It is possible that my language would have evolved similarly without emigration.

VP: *Your poems contain many negative expressions for a believer: I take examples from the book* Last Poems of the Last Century: *'Nobody needs my gift' (p. 5), 'Don't fear, don't complain / do not let despair drown you / no one knows the day, the hour' (p. 8); 'I do not see, do not listen, do not feel' (p. 9); 'No need for words. No need'; 'And nothing to weep over, / nor measure oneself for the coffin' (p. 50); 'No, nothing / to feel sorry, nothing' (p. 71). What is their poetic function?*

NG: Lev Loseff was the first to comment on this in a review of *Alien Stones* (*Chuzhie kamni*). So I suppose there must be something in it. Talking of 'for a believer', consider the poem 'No! It was probably my first cry', from the cycle of eight liners 'Exegi monumentum'. I recently wrote these 'no's, this 'without', this 'rejection of the devil'. Perhaps my 'no' is most clearly expressed in this poem: 'This Russian "No" / in a foreign country...'. I think this appeared in my work or figured largely in it precisely in emigration.

VP: *Sometimes you use a lot of alliteration. Sometimes it is like a veritable storm: 'v mertsayushchikh vysiakh visia' (1963); 'kak shchekot za shchekoi' (1967). What part does the aural dimension play in your work?*

NG: It is very important. The sense of sound or the sound of sense, which I discuss in a review of one of Loseff's books, is for me the very essence, nothing is more important. That is, the sound (alliteration is part of this) gives birth to sense.

VP: *You worked for a long time as deputy editor of the Paris review* Kontinent. *Moreover, from the early 80s until 2001 you worked for a Russian newspaper,* Russkaya mysl. *Tell us about your editorial work for these Russian publications.*

NG: Those were remarkable years. But it would take too long to go into it. *Kontinent* was an openly anti-Communist review – not pretentiously so but in essence, as a cultural opponent to Communism. It published, for example, chapters from Grossman's novels, Felix Kandel's prose. We were the first to publish Yury Maletsky (pseudonymously), and had virtually exclusive rights to Brodsky's poems, Kenzheev, Soprovsky and Gandlevsky, articles and essays on literature. Lev Loseff made a delayed debut in our pages.

VP: *You went to Moscow, on a first visit after your emigration, in December 1992. How did they receive you?*

NG: I was well received. But more recently, I would have been received even better. At the time my loyal readers came, who missed me, but now there are many new fans among the young, even the very young.

VP: *Can poems such as 'From Pindemonti' be read allegorically as comments on contemporary Russian society?*

NG: Why allegorically? It's a realistic description.

NG: *At last your documentary book* Noon (Polden), *which describes the events of 1968, has been published in Russia. Do you think it will alter the consciousness of the young generation of Russian readers?*

NG: Hard to say. Here are some comments in *Zhivoy Zhurnal (Live Journal)* on that topic: 'The seven saved the honour of this great country'; 'They defamed the country, and did not save its honour'; 'The trial of the five (Bogoraz, Litvinov, Delaunay, Babitsky, Dremlyuga) was a special trial (Gorbanevskaya and Fainberg were declared insane). Of each of them one might say: "Behold, the man!'". August 1968 demonstrated that there were gaps in the system and pointed to where they were. It was a real event, which made a huge, if invisible, breach in the Kremlin's walls.

VP: *You have just returned from Russia. How often are you invited?*

NG: Well, I'm off there again tomorrow. That will make the third time this year. Since the beginning of 2005, I have been there twice a year. But this year is the fortieth anniversary of the *Chronicle* and of our demonstration, which is being celebrated.

VP: *What is it you value most in human beings?*

NG: When I value someone, I value the whole, the personality as such. Perhaps it's best, again, to have recourse to negative attributes, to the '*ne*!', so as not to lie, not to kowtow to the general tendency (whatever that may be), hopefully not to use obscenities (although there are exceptions which I can forgive); I imagine there are lots of other 'no's.

Bibliography

Poetry

Stikhi [Poems], Frankfurt: Posev, 1969. Compiled without the knowledge or agreement of the author, including many poems since rejected by her.

Selected Poems, translated and introduced by Daniel Weissbort, Manchester: Carcanet Press, 1972.

Poberezhye [Seaboard], Ann Arbor: Ardis, 1973.

Tri tetradi stikhotvorenii [Three Notebooks of Poems], Bremen: K-Press, 1975. Three consecutive *samizdat* notebooks of poems.

Pereletaya snezhnuyu granitsu [Flying over the Snowy Frontier], Paris: IMKA Press, 1979.

Chuzhie kamni [Alien Stones], New York: Russica Publishers, 1983.

Angel derevianny [Wooden Angel], Ann Abor: Ardis, 1983. Includes *Poberezhye*, plus *Tri tetradi stikhotvorenii*.

Peremennaya oblachnost' [Alternating Clouds], Paris: Kontact, 1986.

Gde i kogda [Where and When], Paris: Kontakt, 1986.

Tsvet vereska [Flower of the Heather], Tenefly (USA): Ermitazh, 1993. Includes *Seventh Book*, not published separately, and *One More*.

I ya zhila-byla [Once Upon a Time]: containing poems written between 1992 and 1994, this was intended as a book, but was never published.

Nabor [Type-setting], Moscow: Argo-Risk, 1996.

Ne spi na zakate. Pochti polnoe isbrannoe [Don't Sleep at Dawn. An Almost Complete Selection], St Petersburg: Liki Rossii, 1996.

Kto o chyom poyot [Who Sings What], Moscow: Argo-Risk, 1998.

13 vos'mistishii i eshche 67 stikhotvorenii [13 Eight-liners and 67 More Poems], Moscow: Argo-Risk/Tver: Kolonna, 2000.

Poslednie stikhi togo veka [Last Poems of the Last Century], Moscow: Argo-Risk/Tver: Kolonna, 2001.

Russko-Russkii razgovor. Izbrannye stikhotvoreniya. Poema bez poemy. Novaya kniga stikhov [Russo-Russian Conversation. Selected Poems. Poem without a Poem. New Book of Poems], Moscow: OGI, 2003.

I togda ia vliubilas' v chuzhie stikhi. Izbrannye perevody iz polskoi poezii [At That Time, I Fell for Foreign Poems. Selected Translations from Polish Poetry], Warsaw: National Library, 2006. Bilingual edition.

Chainaya roza [Tea Rose], Moscow: Novoe literaturnoe obozrenie, 2006.

Krugi po vode [Circles in the Water], Moscow: BaltRus-Novoe literaturnoe obozrenie, 2010.

Razvilki [Forks in the Road], Saratov: NP 'Dom iskusstv', 2010.

Pril'pe zemli dush moia, 1956–2010 [My Soul Cleaveth unto the Dust, 1956–2010], Moscow: Russkii Guliver, 2011.

Shtoito. Stikhi 2010 [Sumthing. Poems 2010], Moscow: Argo-Risk, 2011.

Prose

Polden. Delo o demonstratsii na Krasnoi ploshchadi 25 avgusta 1968 goda [Noon. On the Demonstration in Red Square 25 August 1968], Frankfurt-am-Main: Posev, 1970. Enlarged edition, Moscow: Novoe izdatelstvo, 2007.

Neslomlennaya Pol'sha na stranitsakh 'Russkoi mysli' [Unbroken Poland on the Pages of 'Russian Thought'], Paris: izdanie 'Russkoi mysli', 1984.

Prozoi. O poezii i poetakh [Prose. On Poetry and Poets], Moscow: Russkii Guliver, in press.